Data
Interoperability

Unified Architecture
Connecting All of Your Data

Dave Wells

Technics Publications
SEDONA, ARIZONA

TECHNICS PUBLICATIONS

115 Linda Vista, Sedona, AZ 86336 USA
https://www.TechnicsPub.com

Edited by Steve Hoberman
Cover design by Lorena Molinari

First Printing 2025

Copyright © 2025 by Dave Wells

ISBN, print ed.	9798898160227
ISBN, Kindle ed.	9798898160234
ISBN, PDF ed.	9798898160241

Contents

ONE

The Data Interoperability Imperative

For decades, enterprise data architecture has followed a familiar pattern: when systems need to share data, we copy it. We extract from one place, transform it into the shape another system expects, and write it to a file or load it into a repository designed for that new purpose. Data warehouses, operational data stores, data lakes, and countless point-to-point data flows all owe their existence to this approach.

It works—up to a point. Copy-based integration makes cross-system analysis possible. It supports enterprise reporting, dashboards, and business intelligence (BI). It feeds the analytical platforms that form the backbone of modern decision-making. But as the number of systems grows and the pace of change accelerates, the cracks in this model are hard to ignore. Every new copy adds cost, latency, and complexity. Every schema change ripples through downstream processes. And every independent integration adds to the tangle of one-off solutions that are expensive to maintain and fragile in the face of change.

Over time, this accumulation becomes a form of technical debt: the proliferation of redundant data copies, ad hoc pipelines, and brittle point-to-point connections makes change slow, labor intensive, and with inherently higher risk. Small adjustments may require wide-reaching rework. The architecture grows heavier with each project, until the effort required to maintain the ecosystem begins to outweigh its ability to adapt. Breaking free of that cycle means rethinking how systems exchange data in the first place—shifting from copy-and-transform toward a model built on interoperability.

Interoperability offers another way. Instead of replicating data into new systems, files, and databases to make it usable, interoperability focuses on enabling systems to communicate meaningfully where the data already lives.

It's about shared understanding, not just shared storage.

When systems can interpret each other's data without complex transformations and redundancy by design, the architecture becomes simpler, faster, and more resilient.

The principles aren't new—we've applied them in software integration for years. Common protocols, agreed-upon message formats, and well-defined contracts make it possible for applications built in different eras and languages to exchange information. Data interoperability applies the same thinking to the data itself. A shared semantic foundation lets each system "speak" in its own dialect while still understanding the others.

This doesn't make data integration obsolete. Some use cases still call for consolidated, transformed datasets—especially in analytics. But it does give us a choice. Instead of defaulting to copy-and-transform, we can design for direct, semantically aligned exchange when that's the better fit.

In the chapters ahead, we'll explore the two domains where this choice matters most: operational and analytical data management. Each has its own challenges—sprawl, silos, disparity, and friction—that make meaningful connections difficult. Each has inherited patterns from decades of copy-based integration. And each stands to benefit when interoperability is part of the architectural toolbox.

It's worth noting, though, that the distinction between these domains is not absolute. Operational and analytical are, in many ways, "macro-silos"—broad groupings that describe categories of use cases rather than intrinsic qualities of the data itself. The data in both worlds often comes from the same sources, but we treat it differently based on purpose: one side for running the business, the other for understanding it. Integration efforts tend to stay within domain boundaries—operational with operational, analytical with analytical—leaving the flow of meaning between them underdeveloped. Interoperability can bridge this gap.

Because it works at the semantic level, it can operate across domains as easily as within them, creating a continuum of understanding that blurs the line between operational and analytical. In some cases, that line may even disappear altogether, replaced by a more fluid exchange of data that serves both immediate action and long-term insight.

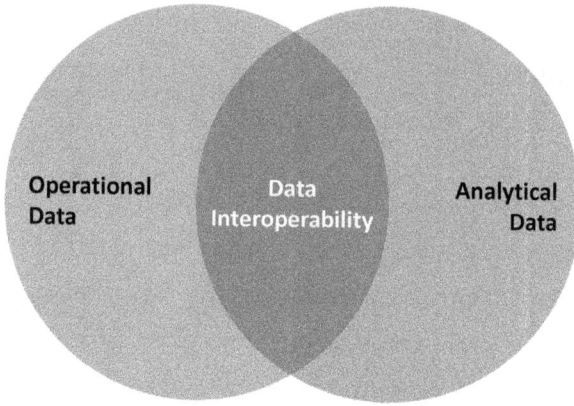

Figure 1: Operational and Analytical Data as Macro-Silos. The operational/analytical distinction is useful to understand how data is used, but it's not an inherent property of the data itself. In practice, these domains function like "macro-silos," each with its own tools, governance patterns, and integration approaches.

To understand the driving forces of the data interoperability imperative, we'll start with operational data because that's where the complexity is most entrenched and the opportunity for interoperability is most immediate. Then we'll turn to analytical data where interoperability can simplify pipelines, improve trust, and speed delivery. Together, these perspectives set the stage for a deeper dive into data interoperability: what it is, how it works, and how to design for it.

TWO

The Operational Data Landscape

In data management, we often talk about the distinction between operational data and analytical data. It's a useful distinction—at least for data and IT professionals. But for most business people, it doesn't mean much. Data is just data. It supports business activities, informs decisions, and keeps things moving—regardless of where it lives or what it's called.

Still, the distinction matters. Not because it changes how business people think, but because it shapes how data is created, managed, and made available. And those things—creation, management, and availability—have real consequences.

Operational data is the day-to-day stuff.

It's generated and updated by the business as it runs—the transactions, interactions, and events that drive sales, fulfill orders, issue invoices, and support customers. It's the data that flows through systems like customer relationship management (CRM), enterprise resource planning (ERP), and point of sale (POS). Fast-moving. High-volume. Deeply embedded in business operations. And usually stored in databases tightly coupled with the systems that create it.

> *Analytical data plays a different role. It's how we observe, understand, and improve the business.*

This is where we find historical records, performance metrics, and business indicators that support decision-making. It's the foundation for analytics of all kinds—descriptive, diagnostic, predictive, and prescriptive. Some of it comes from operational sources, but some of it doesn't. External data, third-party sources, benchmarks, and models all add to the picture. And it's typically stored in data warehouses, data lakes, and other systems designed for analysis, not transactions.

This distinction—operational versus analytical—is more than terminology. It sits at the core of how we design our data environments. It influences architecture. It shapes governance. And it quietly affects the flow of data through the organization, often in ways we don't stop to consider. Business users may not care about the classification, but the consequences of how we treat each kind of data ripple across performance, insight, and even strategy.

It's a foundational idea in modern data architecture. But like many foundations, it's worth revisiting now and then—especially when the world around it is changing.

A Second Look at Operational and Analytical Data

Most of us in data management have heard—and probably repeated—the familiar distinction between operational data and analytical data. It's almost a mantra. But how often do we stop to think about what that distinction really means, especially from the perspective of enterprise architecture? And more importantly, what does that distinction miss?

> *We like to say that operational data is for running the business and analytical data is for observing it. Clean, simple, and technically true. But here's the problem: the real world of business isn't clean or simple. It's messy, interconnected, and full of nuance. And in the real world, that tidy separation between operational and analytical data doesn't always hold up.*

Operational Systems: The Data Workhorses

Operational systems are the places where data is born. They create it, they update it, and they use it every day. Think CRM, ERP, logistics, billing, call centers—these systems are busy. They're the heartbeat of the business. Most of the data we rely on starts here, and a lot of it stays here, circulating quietly through daily transactions and workflows.

But operational systems don't live in isolation. They rarely do one thing or serve one audience. They need to connect, share, and cooperate with other systems. Sales needs data from marketing. Fulfillment needs data from orders. Billing needs data from just about everyone. The idea that each function can operate in a vacuum is a myth. Business doesn't work that way—and neither should data.

That interconnectedness sounds good in theory. But in practice? It's hard. Different systems were built at different times by different teams, each with its own naming conventions, structures, and assumptions. The same customer might be stored three times under three different schemas. And good luck trying to link them without serious effort. That's where we hit the wall—integration isn't just difficult, it's persistently difficult.

We wrestle with overlapping data. We struggle to make sense of inconsistencies. And we spend enormous time and effort just trying to connect the dots. This is the world of operational data— a world where interoperability isn't a buzzword, it's a battlefield.

The Comfort of Analytical Data

So, what did we do about this messy operational world? For years, the answer was simple: we avoided it.

Rather than fix the problems at the source, we copied the data. We treated operational systems as raw material, piped the data into warehouses and lakes, cleaned it up a bit (or a lot), and used those cleaned-up copies for analysis. We gave it new names—BI, dashboards, metrics—and convinced ourselves that this was the smart way to manage data.

And to be fair, it was smart. It worked. It gave us insights we didn't have before. It made analysis possible, and often even powerful.

But let's be honest—we also got a little too comfortable. We got used to treating analytical systems as the "real" source of truth, even though they were two steps removed from the actual business. We prioritized data quality for dashboards, but let chaos rule in the systems that actually run the business.

And now, that model is showing its age. We live in a world that demands speed, adaptability, and real-time decision-making. Waiting for overnight ETL jobs and stale metrics isn't good enough anymore. Business users want insight at the point of action, not the point of reporting. And that means we need to rethink the way data flows through the organization—not just for analytics, but for operations too.

The Interoperability Imperative

This brings us to an uncomfortable but necessary truth: the traditional separation of operational and analytical data has become an architectural crutch. It helped us manage complexity. It helped us get things done. But it also kept us from solving the harder problem—making our systems and databases work together.

> That's what interoperability is all about. Not just connecting systems, but making sure they understand each other. Sharing data in a way that's meaningful, consistent, and trustworthy—not just extractable. And doing it without waiting for a downstream cleanup crew.

It's not easy. It means facing the hard realities of legacy systems, semantic mismatches, and conflicting assumptions. But it's also necessary. Because if we want our businesses to be fast, smart, and resilient, we can't keep treating operational integration as someone else's problem.

There's a lot of talk these days about data mesh, data fabric, and real-time pipelines. These aren't just trendy terms—they're signs that the industry is waking up to the need for connected operations, not just better reports.

> The future of data management isn't just in the lake.
> It's in the bloodstream of the business.

Expanding the View of Operational Systems

If we want to truly interconnect operational data—and not just talk about it—we need to start by expanding our view of what operational systems actually are. Too often, when we hear the phrase "operational systems," our minds immediately go to transactional systems—the OLTP engines that record the basics of business activity. And yes, they're important. In many organizations, they're still the largest, most visible part of the operational landscape.

Transactional systems are the systems of record. They capture what happened: the order that was placed, the invoice that was sent, the payment that was received. They're the backbone for tracking sales, purchases, inventory, and payroll—the essential functions that every business needs to run.

But they're not the whole story. Not anymore.

Today's operational environments are broader and more complex than they used to be.

Workflow automation systems are now a critical part of how work gets done. These systems manage the flow of approvals, route documents, enable electronic signatures, and replace the burden of manual, paper-based processes. They don't always get the same attention as transactional systems, but they play a vital role in keeping business processes moving efficiently—and they generate a steady stream of operational data along the way.

In manufacturing environments, the picture gets even richer. Manufacturing automation systems control machines, coordinate robotics, monitor performance, and schedule preventive maintenance. These systems aren't just operational—they are the operation. Without them, modern manufacturing would grind to a halt. And the data they produce—about throughput, uptime, quality, and performance—is as operational as it gets.

Then there's the world of IoT—which continues to grow, diversify, and accelerate. We now see smart buildings, connected vehicles, real-time tracking systems, and embedded sensors in everything from factory floors to delivery vans. IoT systems monitor environments, detect conditions, and trigger automated responses. Some are commercial—building management systems, smart parking, and energy monitoring. Others are industrial— real-time telemetry, safety systems, predictive maintenance, and supply chain visibility. These systems continuously capture data at the edge and feed it into the operational flow of the business.

What do all of these systems have in common? They are operational—not just in the technical sense, but in the business sense. They are integral to how work gets done. They produce data, consume data, and depend on data to function. And yet, they are often overlooked when we talk about operational data, because they don't fit neatly into the old OLTP mold.

> *If we want operational data to be connected, consistent,*
> *and trustworthy, we need to recognize the full landscape.*

That means acknowledging that operational systems come in many forms—and that all of them contribute to the complexity we face in managing and integrating operational data. Transactional systems may still be the core, but they're no longer alone.

Understanding the Operational Systems Portfolio

When we step back and look at the broader picture, a clearer structure begins to emerge. From a functional standpoint, we can categorize operational systems into five major types:

- **Transactional systems**—the traditional backbone, handling day-to-day business transactions.
- **Workflow automation systems**—streamlining processes, tracking activity, and eliminating paper.
- **Manufacturing automation systems**—controlling equipment, robotics, and industrial processes.
- **Commercial IoT systems**—managing the environment through smart infrastructure.
- **Industrial IoT systems**—capturing real-time signals from the physical world for automation and response.

It's a useful framework—five types, each playing a different role in how the business runs. But function is only one lens. When we shift our focus to system origin—where these systems come from, how they were built, and how they've evolved—we introduce another layer of complexity. And that complexity is key to understanding why connecting operational data remains such a persistent challenge.

	Legacy	Custom	ERP	Web	SaaS	Mobile
Transactional Systems	✓	✓	✓	✓	✓	✓
Workflow Automation		✓	✓	✓	✓	
Manufacturing Automation	✓				✓	✓
Commercial IoT				✓	✓	
Industrial IoT				✓	✓	✓

Figure 2: The Operational Systems Portfolio.

Start with the legacy systems—the oldest residents in the operational landscape. Many were developed in-house years or decades ago, built on technologies that are now outdated, unsupported, or simply inflexible. They're still running, still critical, and still hard to change. In many cases, they're black boxes—systems that work, but not systems we can easily peer into or connect with.

Then there are custom applications—systems developed more recently, often tailored to meet specific business needs. Unlike legacy systems, these tend to be more modern and somewhat easier to modify. But like their older cousins, they are often built in isolation. Functional integration and data integration are rarely part of the design. That makes them just as prone to fragmentation.

ERP systems offer something different—a suite of integrated applications designed to work together. Within the boundaries of a single ERP platform, you often get reliable data integration and consistency. But step outside those boundaries and the challenge returns. ERPs are notoriously difficult to extend or integrate with external systems, especially if the external systems don't speak the same language.

And of course, technology hasn't stood still. Today's operational environments increasingly include web-based, Software as a Service (SaaS), and mobile applications. These systems often come with integration features—application programming interfaces (APIs), webhooks, and plug-and-play connectors. But the extent of that integration depends heavily on the mix of systems in place. Some vendors make interoperability a priority. Others leave it up to the customer to stitch things together manually.

What we end up with is a portfolio of systems that spans a wide range—from legacy to mobile, from monolithic to modular, from integrated suites to disconnected tools. And unfortunately, disconnect and disparity are more common than integration and interoperability.

Transactional systems, in particular, cut across all these categories. You'll find them everywhere—legacy mainframes, custom internal apps, ERP modules, web-based tools, SaaS platforms, and mobile apps. They're pervasive. And they're often the hardest to connect, precisely because they're so varied in origin and structure.

Workflow automation systems tend to sit toward the newer end of the spectrum—mostly custom-built or SaaS-based. Manufacturing automation can go either way. Older plants still run on legacy systems. Newer operations may rely on SaaS and mobile apps. IoT systems are largely web-driven, with SaaS platforms and mobile dashboards handling data collection and control.

So what does all this mean?

It means that most organizations are managing a portfolio of operational systems that is diverse, fragmented, and functionally siloed. The systems don't talk to each other. The data isn't aligned. And the people who rely on that data are often forced to work around the gaps—manually reconciling records, re-entering information, or making decisions without a full picture.

The variety, diversity, disparity, and widespread lack of system-to-system connection—these are the defining traits of today's operational systems environment. They are also the biggest barriers to delivering connected, consistent, and trusted operational data.

Until we confront these realities and develop strategies to address them, our data management practices will continue to fall short—especially when it comes to operational integration.

Management Challenges of Operational Systems

Among all the challenges in managing operational systems, two stand out as both the most obvious and the most persistent: interoperability and integration. These issues are front and center because they strike at the heart of what it means for systems to work together—or more often, not work together.

At the core, these are challenges of connecting disparate data. Integration works around the problems of disparity, addressing symptoms by resolving differences at the schema level. Interoperability is different. It tackles disparity at the semantic level, addressing causes of data disconnects with shared meaning instead of shared schema.

The reality is that these challenges span the entire systems continuum, from legacy mainframes to modern mobile apps. It doesn't matter whether the system was built 30 years ago or deployed last week—making systems talk to one another is hard. The technologies may be different, but the pain is surprisingly consistent.

With legacy systems, the biggest issues are maintenance and support. These systems often run on aging infrastructure, use outdated programming languages, and lack documentation. Changing them is difficult. Integrating them is worse. They weren't designed to connect to anything outside themselves—and it shows.

Custom-built applications tend to be easier to support than legacy systems, but they bring their own challenges—especially if they were developed without an integration strategy in mind. These systems often function well on their own, but they're not built to play nicely with others. They may use idiosyncratic data models or one-off interfaces that make interoperability brittle at best.

ERP systems offer more promise. They were built for integration—at least within their own ecosystems. The challenge here is that ERP integration tends to stop at the ERP boundary. Connecting an ERP to anything else—especially if it's custom or cloud-based—still requires significant effort.

Then there's the newer end of the spectrum: web-based systems, SaaS platforms, and mobile apps. At first glance, these systems seem more flexible. Many offer APIs, integration hooks, and third-party connectors. But don't let the gloss fool you—these systems come with their own issues. Maintenance is still a challenge, especially when dealing with rapid vendor updates or shifting APIs. Support structures are fragmented. And hybrid deployments—with parts of the system on-premises, other parts in the cloud, and still others accessed via mobile—introduce a whole new level of architectural complexity.

> *The more systems we have, the more moving parts we introduce. And the more moving parts we introduce, the harder it becomes to keep everything in sync. Change becomes more difficult. Maintenance becomes more fragile. And integration becomes a moving target.*

It's not just about connection points either. Semantic differences and data model variations run across all systems, regardless of origin. What one system calls a customer, another might call a client, or an account, or a contact. Even when two systems seem similar, the underlying assumptions are often different. These misalignments are subtle—and they're everywhere. They are the root causes of the data disconnects that frustrate users and complicate analytics.

And we haven't even mentioned hybrid environments—those messy combinations of on-prem, cloud, and mobile where some systems are owned, some are rented, and some are effectively black boxes. Trying to make sense of data across those boundaries is like trying to assemble a puzzle where every piece comes from a different manufacturer.

So yes—the challenges are many. So much variation. So many systems, speaking so many dialects of data. Trying to pull it all together, to make it work as one cohesive whole—it's no wonder this continues to be one of the most difficult and expensive aspects of enterprise data management.

And yet, one of the biggest reasons we struggle is surprisingly basic: most organizations lack a well-thought-out, clearly designed, and properly documented operational data architecture.

We have architecture for analytics. We have blueprints for warehouses, lakes, and dashboards. But for operational systems—the very systems that generate, process, and act on the data—we often work without a map. It's hard to build connected systems when you don't know what you're connecting. It's even harder to manage data across systems when no one's responsible for seeing the full picture.

Until that changes, integration will continue to be reactive, patchwork, and painful—not because we lack the technology, but because we lack the foundation.

What Happened to Operational Data Architecture?

If we want to make real progress with interoperability—not just temporary fixes, but lasting capability—then we have to take a hard look at operational data architecture. And not just take a look—we need to restore it to the priority level it once had. Because without it, the operational data challenges we've been talking about will persist. No amount of clever integration or patchwork APIs will solve a problem that starts at the architectural level.

The strange thing is, operational data architecture wasn't always an afterthought. In fact, there was a time—back in the 1970s and 80s—when it was front and center. The focus then was enterprise data management, and the systems we had were largely operational. Business computing was about getting work done— processing transactions, managing inventory, and producing reports. The architecture was designed around those operational needs. Data was modeled, managed, and governed at the operational level.

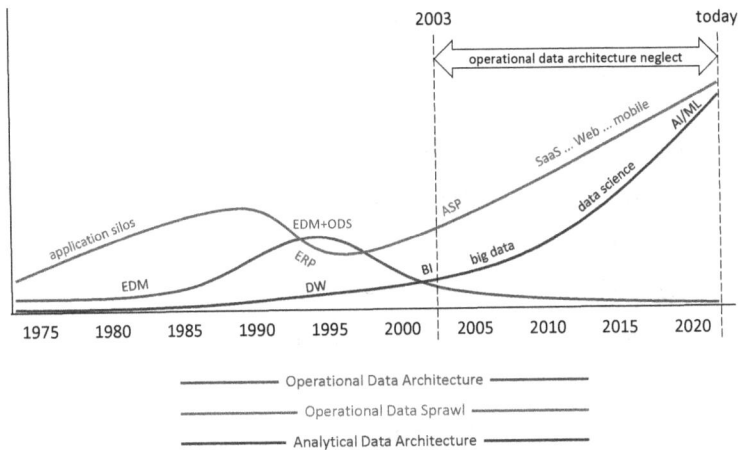

Figure 3: Operational Data Architecture Neglect.

Then things began to shift. In the mid-1990s, the operational data store (ODS) emerged—serving as a middle layer between operational systems and analytical environments. The ODS was a clever idea: take some of the principles of data warehousing—

mainly integration and transformation—and apply them to current, operational data. For a brief moment, attention swung back toward operational data architecture.

But it didn't last.

The ODS was often viewed as an interim solution—a staging area, a feeder layer, a technical convenience. And soon, attention moved elsewhere. The rise of data warehousing in the late 90s, followed by the explosion of business intelligence in the early 2000s, shifted the architectural conversation away from operations and toward analytics. That focus only deepened with the arrival of big data, data science, and today's fascination with AI and machine learning. Analytical architecture became the hot topic. Operational architecture quietly faded into the background.

Meanwhile, something else was happening—something big. Operational data was sprawling. What used to be a relatively stable set of internal systems began to spread. First into ERP platforms that claimed to centralize everything, then out again into application service providers, and later into SaaS, web-based tools, and mobile apps. The operational environment wasn't shrinking—it was exploding. More systems. More vendors. More places where data could live, change, and flow.

Now we find ourselves in an unusual position. Just as operational data became more fragmented, more distributed, and more difficult to manage, our attention to operational data architecture all but disappeared.

We shouldn't be surprised that we're struggling.

The truth is, we've spent the past two decades investing heavily in analytical data architecture—and with good reason. Data warehousing helped standardize reporting. BI tools brought insight closer to decision-makers. Big data and data science unlocked new value. And now, with AI and machine learning, we're pushing the boundaries of what data can do.

But in the process, we've neglected the data that runs the business—the operational data that fuels everything from transactions to customer service to real-time response. We've assumed it would take care of itself. We've treated integration as a technical afterthought. And we've forgotten that without a solid architectural foundation, operational data will always be fragile, fragmented, and hard to trust.

We've built sophisticated towers of insight on top of a shaky, uneven base.

It's time to fix the foundation. Many of the operational challenges we face today—fragmented systems, disconnected data, semantic mismatches, and brittle integration—stem from one core issue: the absence of a well-defined operational data architecture. Most organizations simply don't have one. Or if they do, it's little more than a diagram of systems with arrows between them—not a thoughtfully designed, well-documented framework for how operational data should flow, be governed, and evolve. As a result, every new system adds to the complexity. Every integration effort feels custom. Every attempt to adapt becomes reactive, expensive, and slow. Without a clear architectural foundation, interoperability becomes an uphill battle—not because it's impossible, but because it's unplanned.

Managing Operational Data

Operational data management should be purposeful. That may sound obvious, but too often we approach it as a technical necessity rather than a strategic discipline. We manage what we have, respond to what's broken, and patch what's under pressure—without stepping back to ask what we're actually trying to accomplish.

> *Purpose gets replaced by process.*
> *Goals give way to habits.*

But effective operational data management isn't just about keeping systems running or reports accurate. It's about managing data with specific objectives in mind—clear outcomes that solve real problems and move the organization forward. That kind of purposeful management starts by recognizing the challenges we're up against. Not just the daily annoyances or localized issues, but the systemic patterns that create friction, fragmentation, and frustration across the enterprise.

I focus on five major challenges that show up in nearly every organization. They're not new problems, but they're often overlooked, underestimated, or misunderstood:

- **Data sprawl**—the unchecked growth of data sources and systems.
- **Data silos**—the isolation of data within departments, tools, or platforms.
- **Data disparity**—the inconsistencies in structure, semantics, and quality.
- **Data friction**—the difficulty of getting data where it's needed, when it's needed.
- **Global data**—the added complexity of operating across regions, languages, and regulations.

Each of these challenges creates real obstacles. Together, they create something much bigger—a state I call data chaos. And that, ultimately, is the biggest challenge of all.

Data chaos shows up in a thousand small ways: conflicting numbers, missing records, duplicate entries, endless reconciliation, and constant rework. But at its core, data chaos is what happens when operational data becomes so scattered, inconsistent, and difficult to manage that we can no longer rely on it to run the business.

The goal of operational data management is to overcome that chaos—not just temporarily, and not just in pockets, but systematically and sustainably. To do that, we have to take each of the contributing challenges seriously. We have to understand them, name them, and then take deliberate steps to resolve them.

Data Sprawl: When Everything is Everywhere

We'll begin with data sprawl—because it's usually where the trouble starts.

Data sprawl is the uncontrolled and accelerating expansion of data—in every direction, across every platform, and through every imaginable process. It's the result of how we create, collect, store, copy, share, and use data—and the many, many ways that we now deploy databases and data management systems.

We create data constantly—through transaction systems, websites, mobile apps, IoT devices, and sensors. We collect it not only from internal operations, but also from partners, vendors, third-party providers, and purchased sources. Social media, clickstreams, logs, APIs, scraped content—the list keeps growing. The ways we bring data in are almost limitless. So are the sources.

And once we collect it, we store it—but not in any one place, and certainly not in any one format. Yes, relational databases are still common, but their dominance is fading fast. Data lives in spreadsheets—and there are probably more spreadsheets out there than anyone really wants to admit. We also store data in NoSQL databases, flat files, JSON and XML documents, CSV exports, unstructured blobs, and plain text. The sheer variety of storage formats is staggering.

We also copy it—and copy it again. We move data into data lakes, data warehouses, operational data stores, master data hubs, and all manner of downstream environments. We make staging copies, backup copies, reference copies, and audit copies. Sometimes, we can no longer tell which is the source and which is the copy. And somewhere along the way, we lose track of what changed, who made the change, or why it was copied in the first place.

We use data in many ways, but tend to focus most of our attention on analytics—the data science models, dashboards, and BI tools that support high-level insights. That's important, of course. But we forget that some of the most critical uses of operational data are far more routine—audit trails, exception reports, transactional reconciliation, and daily logs. The everyday stuff that keeps the business running.

And we haven't even talked about where we deploy all of this. On-premises infrastructure still plays a role, but more and more data is moving to the cloud—or, more accurately, multiple clouds. Some systems are hybrid, with parts in the data center and parts in public cloud environments. Others are spread across vendors, regions, and architectures. It's no longer uncommon to find a single business process supported by systems deployed in three or more places, on three or more platforms. So we have this vast, scattered, constantly growing universe of operational data:

- Data created in a dozen different ways,
- Collected from hundreds of sources,
- Stored in who-knows-how-many formats,
- Copied and shared across layers of infrastructure,
- Used by people who may or may not understand its origin or context,
- And deployed across a patchwork of on-prem, cloud, and hybrid environments.

This is data sprawl. It's not just about scale—it's about fragmentation without structure. It's about expansion without architecture. And it's one of the biggest reasons why operational data has become so difficult to manage, integrate, and trust.

> *Until we recognize and address data sprawl as a real and present challenge, every other operational data problem becomes harder. And every attempt at interoperability will be one more patch on an ever-expanding surface.*

Data Silos: Islands of Information

If data sprawl is about too much data in too many places, data silos are about data being boxed in—confined within boundaries that were never meant to be crossed.

A data silo is what happens when a data repository is defined, controlled, and managed entirely within the scope of a single business unit, function, process, or system. It's a local database, often optimized for local use, with its own structure, its own terminology, and its own rules. And because it's built to serve a narrow purpose, it rarely considers how that data might be used—or needed—elsewhere.

Every business function tends to speak its own language. Sales talks about leads, opportunities, and close rates. Finance talks about GL codes, accruals, and revenue recognition. Manufacturing, HR, logistics—each has its own data vocabulary, its own way of modeling the world. And when each of those functions builds or buys its own systems, it also builds or buys its own version of the truth.

The result? A collection of disconnected systems, each holding a small part of the enterprise story—but none of them offering the full picture.

Data silos are everywhere. They show up in ERP modules that don't fully communicate. In SaaS applications that don't play well with others. In custom-built tools that were never designed for integration. Even in spreadsheets tucked away on personal drives, managing small-but-critical data that no one else knows about.

And the consequences are familiar:

- Redundant data entry.
- Conflicting numbers.
- Endless reconciliation.
- Manual workarounds to bridge gaps between systems.

It's no surprise that data silos have become the driving force behind data warehousing and enterprise data integration efforts. Data warehousing, at its core, is about reaching into these silos, extracting what's useful, transforming it to align with other data, and bringing it all together for analytical use.

That's a big step forward. But here's the thing: while data warehousing helps solve the analytical side of the silo problem, it does very little to address operational data silos. The data warehouse may help us understand what happened, but it doesn't help operational systems talk to one another in real time. It doesn't eliminate redundancy. It doesn't harmonize terminology across live processes. It doesn't create shared understanding at the point of action.

So the silos remain—in the daily operation of the business. In the systems that generate the data. In the processes that depend on it. And in the people who make decisions without full visibility.

Overcoming data silos means rethinking how we structure systems, how we define data, and how we encourage cross-functional data sharing—not just in our analytical layers, but where the work is actually being done.

Data Disparity: When the Pieces Don't Fit

Data silos lead to data disparity. Once data is boxed in, managed in isolation, and shaped by narrow perspectives, it's only a matter of time before the differences begin to surface—and cause real problems.

Data disparity is the term we use to describe these differences— the conflicts and inconsistencies in data content, structure, semantics, and meaning. It's not just a formatting issue or a naming mismatch. It's something deeper. Data disparity is what happens when two systems hold data about the same thing, but manage it in fundamentally different ways.

These disparities are often invisible at first glance. They live in column names, business rules, assumptions, and metadata—and they show up at the worst possible times. A customer record in one system includes a billing contact. In another, it includes multiple locations. In a third, it tracks nothing but loyalty points. Each system is technically "right" in its own context—but taken together, they paint a fragmented and conflicting picture.

And that leads directly to miscommunication, misunderstanding, and mistrust. People don't trust data when it doesn't line up. They waste time resolving discrepancies. They argue about whose numbers are correct. And they begin to rely on side processes, extracts, and personal workarounds—which only make the problem worse.

To underscore the seriousness of the issue, it helps to go back to the root of the word disparate. The American Heritage Dictionary defines it as "fundamentally distinct or different in kind; entirely dissimilar." Merriam-Webster adds: "containing or made up of fundamentally different and often incongruous elements." And that word—incongruous—is key. It means incompatible. Things that don't belong together. Things that simply don't fit.

That's the reality of data disparity. It's not just about different systems holding different data. It's about systems holding conflicting representations of the same concept—managed differently, defined differently, and understood differently by different parts of the business.

> *And when the pieces don't fit, the business suffers.*
> *Insight suffers. Trust suffers.*

Resolving data disparity takes more than just integration. It takes alignment—of definitions, of meanings, of expectations. It takes governance, design, and communication. And it starts by recognizing that even though systems may be connected, their data might not be.

Data Friction: When Data Gets in the Way

Data friction happens when working with data becomes harder than it should be—when the effort required to make sense of the data outweighs the value it provides.

It's what happens when data sprawl, data silos, and data disparity start interfering with people's ability to get the answers they need.

The result is a mix of questions, confusion, frustration, and uncertainty. And eventually, people stop trusting the data altogether. This cartoon tells the story.

Figure 4: Data Friction: Data as a Barrier to Information.

The question seems simple enough:
"How has the customer count changed month over month?"

But the answers are anything but simple:
"We have more than 5,000 new customers in the pipeline."
"We processed orders for 1,700 new customers."
"We closed sales for nearly 2,000 new customers."
"Looks like we lost several customers due to complaints."

And just like that, we're stuck. Too many places with data about customer acquisition and attrition. Too many numbers. Too many ways of counting. And no way to get an answer that inspires confidence. In situations like this, the most common response isn't a better analysis—it's surrender.

"Forget the data! Can you work with a rough estimate?"

That's what data friction looks like. A perfectly reasonable business question derailed by inconsistencies, confusion, and disagreement about what the data actually means.

Here's the real problem: customer count—the very thing we're trying to measure—isn't clearly defined. Beyond that, we have three references to "new customers"—from sales pipeline, closed sales, and processed orders—and there's a good chance each one defines "new customer" differently. We end up debating definitions instead of making decisions.

This is how friction builds. And when the data can't be trusted, people stop using it. They find workarounds. They rely on gut feel. They turn to spreadsheets, shadow systems, or manual methods that feel more controllable— even when they're less reliable.

That's not just frustrating. It is a real data management problem. Data friction breaks down confidence. It slows down decisions. It drives people away from the very systems we've invested in. And worst of all, it reinforces the idea that data isn't worth the trouble—that it's easier to work around it than to work with it. If data is going to support the business, it has to work for the people who use it and that means reducing friction.

Global Data: The Geography of Complexity

Global data is a different kind of challenge. Unlike data sprawl, silos, disparity, or friction—which tend to arise from internal complexity—global data problems are rooted in geography, culture, and regulation. But for global organizations, and for anyone working with data that crosses national borders or regional boundaries, these challenges are just as real—and just as difficult to ignore.

When data spans countries, languages, time zones, and legal frameworks, everything gets more complicated. Data management processes that work reasonably well in a single-region environment often begin to break down. We see it in areas as basic and important as:

- Address validation and formatting
- Matching and standardizing names
- Currency conversion
- Unit translation and measurement
- Time zone alignment
- Regulatory compliance

Data quality becomes harder. Master data management becomes messier. And governance, especially for privacy and protection, becomes far more complex. Regulations vary not just by where data is located, but also by where it's accessed and used. What's compliant in one country may be a violation in another—and that's not a small problem when data flows freely across systems and borders.

Even simple things get complicated. Dates and times need to be reconciled across time zones. Two events recorded at "10:00 AM" in different systems may not have happened at the same time—and that can matter more than we expect.

Currency is another ongoing challenge. With over 50 currencies in active global use—and with exchange rates that change constantly—expressing transaction values in a common unit of measure is never as simple as applying a standard conversion. Time becomes a key factor. What exchange rate should be used? The one from the time of purchase? Of delivery? Of settlement? And what if rates shift significantly between those moments?

Units of measure are slightly more predictable—but still require careful handling. Converting weights, distances, volumes, and temperatures between systems is usually straightforward, but we still run into problems with rounding, local display preferences, and differences in expected units.

And then there's addresses. Global address data lacks a universal standard. In some countries, addressing conventions are well-defined and highly structured. In others, they're informal, ambiguous, or inconsistent. Postal codes vary in format and use. Even the concept of what defines a "valid address" differs from region to region.

Phone numbers pose similar issues—with widely varying formats and no consistent global standard beyond the country code. Names—both for people and for businesses—bring their own set of challenges. Name order, character sets, and naming conventions vary across cultures. And business names often carry legal meaning: Inc., LLC, Ltd., GmbH, AG—each with implications about the entity's structure and jurisdiction.

All of these details matter. They affect data matching, integration, validation, and reporting. They affect customer experience. And they can affect compliance and legal risk.

Working with global data isn't just a technical task. It's a specialized skill set—one that combines knowledge of data structure with understanding of cultural context, business practices, and regulatory environments. Achieving consistency with global data requires not only tools and systems, but also people who know how to manage complexity across borders. And for organizations operating on a global scale, this isn't optional. It's a core part of making operational data usable, trustworthy, and fit for purpose—wherever in the world that purpose may be.

Data Chaos: When it all Comes Apart

When we step back and look at the big picture—data sprawl, data silos, data disparity, data friction, and the added complexity of global data—it becomes clear that we're not just dealing with isolated problems. We're dealing with the collective effect of all these issues working together. And that effect is something I call data chaos.

Data chaos is the condition that emerges when many systems and applications manage their data independently, without coordination, without shared definitions, and without concern for how their data interacts with anyone else's. Each application is doing its own thing—collecting data, storing it, shaping it—in a way that makes sense locally, but causes confusion globally.

It's a model built on local control without systemic coordination. And that model gets messy fast.

Think about it: most organizations today rely on dozens, sometimes hundreds of operational systems. Even a small to mid-size company can have 100 or more. But let's keep it simple and just look at 16. That's a relatively small number—and still more than enough to illustrate the point.

Let's say our business operations depend on 16 applications:

Marketing	Inventory
Call center	Accounts receivable
Employee benefits	Payroll
Order processing	Receiving
Billing	E-commerce
Human resources	Shipping
Sales	Purchasing
Warranty service	Accounts payable

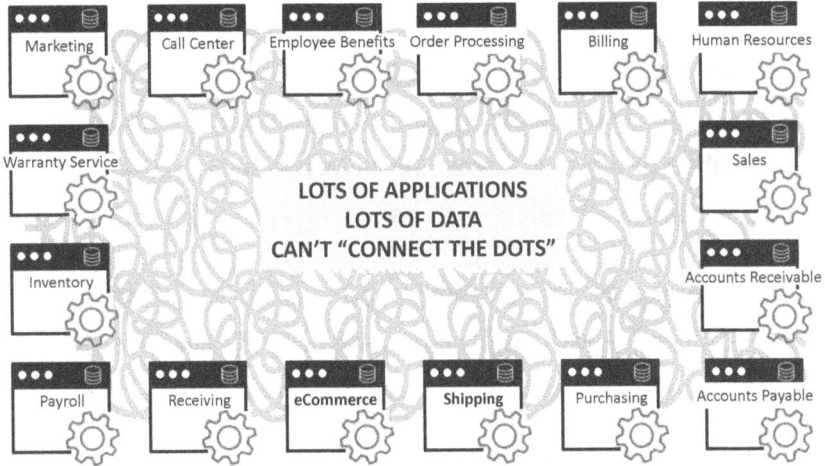

Figure 5: The Nature of Data Chaos.

These aren't edge cases. They're core business functions. And none of them can exist in isolation.

- Sales needs to talk to order processing.
- Order processing needs to talk to billing.
- Billing needs to talk to accounts receivable.
- Order processing needs to talk to shipping.
- Inventory needs to talk to purchasing.
- Purchasing needs to talk to accounts payable.
- Employee benefits needs to talk to payroll.
- Payroll needs to talk to HR.
- HR needs to talk to employee benefits.
- Marketing needs to talk to sales.
- Call center needs to talk to warranty service.

And so on.

With just 16 applications, you could easily have over 100 inter-application dependencies. The actual number might be a bit lower depending on how tightly things are coupled—but it's still big. Big enough to be a real challenge. Big enough that trying to connect the dots across all of those systems becomes a full-time job.

Now, imagine those applications managing their data independently—each with its own data models, business rules, naming conventions, and assumptions. Add in the mix of technologies—legacy systems, custom apps, SaaS platforms, and spreadsheets. Throw in different deployment models—cloud, on-prem, hybrid. Mix in global data complexity.

It's no wonder so many organizations struggle. That's data chaos.

Not because anyone intended it that way. But because we never took a step back to manage operational data systemically and architecturally, rather than as a loosely connected collection of systems and datasets. Without coordination, complexity takes over. And when complexity takes over, consistency breaks down.

> *That's when trust in data begins to erode—*
> *and business decisions are made on guesswork, instinct,*
> *or workarounds.*

And the problem doesn't stop at the number of applications or the connections between them. It gets even more complicated when you consider the mix of application types involved.

Some of the systems in play are part of an ERP suite—designed to integrate, but only within their own boundaries. Others are SaaS applications, each with its own cloud-based logic, data structure, and limitations. Still others are legacy systems, often inflexible and poorly documented. Add to that a layer of web applications, custom-built tools, and mobile apps, and you end up with a patchwork of systems that were never meant to work together.

Each application has its own local database, its own assumptions, and its own idea of what the data means. That's the stuff of data silos, data disparity, and data sprawl—all rolled into one.

And when those systems need to communicate with each other? It's rarely clean or standardized. Instead, what we get is custom-crafted data connections—one-off solutions for each system-to-system communication need. Point-to-point pipelines. Manual handoffs. Local scripts. Spreadsheets emailed back and forth. All of it done in isolation, without a cohesive plan.

The result is a tangle of:

- Overlapping and redundant data
- Inconsistent naming and terminology
- Local definitions that don't align
- Different encodings for the same values
- Varying levels of data quality
- And systems that simply don't share well

Even basic facts—like a customer ID, an order status, or a product description—may be expressed differently from one system to the next. One stores dates as strings. Another uses a different timezone. One counts "active" customers differently than the others. And no one really agrees on what "new" means.

Trying to navigate all of this—to trace dependencies, reconcile differences, and connect the dots—is like wandering through a maze without a map. There's no clear direction. No reliable guide. Just twists, turns, and surprises at every corner. And all of it leads to more rework, more errors, and more frustration. Not just for IT or data teams, but for business users who depend on that data to do their jobs—and often end up building workarounds to avoid dealing with the mess.

This is what unmanaged operational data looks like. And this is exactly why purposeful operational data management isn't just a nice-to-have—it's an organizational imperative. Data chaos isn't just a technical problem. It's an organizational problem. And it's a business risk. The good news ... it's a manageable problem if we choose to face it head-on.

The Typical Response: Point-to-Point Pile-Up

When faced with data chaos—disorganized, disconnected, inconsistent data scattered across a landscape of mismatched applications—the natural response is to start connecting the dots, one at a time. It sounds like a logical approach. We have applications that need to communicate, so we build communication pathways. The problem is how we build them.

Because of data sprawl, data silos, and data disparity, every app-to-app communication becomes a unique, custom-crafted data flow. And the result is a growing web of point-to-point data feeds—each one tailored for a specific use, tied to a specific interface, and tightly coupled to a specific pair of systems.

Need order processing to talk to shipping? Build a feed.
Need shipping to talk to e-commerce? Build another feed.
Need payroll to sync with HR? Build a feed.

And on it goes.

Each of these data flows is built independently, often by different teams using different tools. Each has its own logic, its own schedule or trigger, and its own assumptions about how the data is structured and what it means. The more systems we have—and the more data they need to exchange—the more of these one-off feeds we create.

And with that comes the hidden cost:

- More scheduling complexity
- More opportunity for failure
- More manual coordination
- And more fragility every time something changes

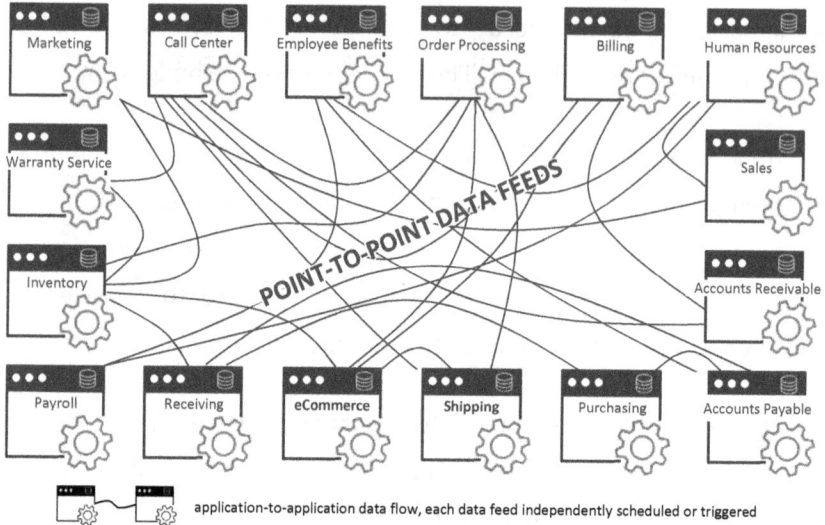

Figure 6: Typical Response to Data Chaos.

What happens when one application sends data to another—and then backs out its transaction? What happens when a feed fails mid-process? How do you prevent a small upstream error from rippling through half a dozen downstream systems?

These are the everyday questions that trap data teams in a reactive cycle. They're not dealing with innovation. They're dealing with recovery. With exceptions. With rollback procedures, error handling, and reconciliation scripts just to keep things from falling apart.

And then comes change—because change is constant.

A SaaS vendor releases a new version and changes how a value is encoded. An ERP system is patched and the schema shifts. A mobile app is updated and now expects different sync logic.

Every change forces a question: What breaks? What feeds are affected? What needs to be rewritten? What downstream reports, dashboards, or systems will now show the wrong data—or no data at all?

This is how technical debt accumulates—quietly, steadily, and expensively.

Each feed is a bit of custom code. Each reconciliation rule is another bit of logic embedded somewhere. The more you build, the more you have to maintain. And the more tightly these pieces are woven together, the more fragile the entire system becomes.

And eventually, the weight of change, complexity, and inconsistency becomes too great. The system can't evolve without breaking something. Every new project takes longer than expected. Every upgrade is a risk. Every improvement feels like a workaround.

This isn't just inefficient. It's unsustainable.

And it's why purposeful, coordinated operational data management must replace this reactive, point-to-point model. Not just to reduce failure, but to make change manageable—and to finally bring structure to the mess. That structure doesn't come from more code or more quick fixes. It comes from architecture—the foundation that organizes data, systems, and integration into something cohesive, intentional, and built to last.

THREE

The Analytical Data Landscape

Analytical data management has always been a moving target. We've chased innovation for decades—from early enterprise data warehouses to Hadoop-based data lakes, from lakehouse architectures to today's talk of data mesh, fabric, and AI-ready platforms. At every stage, we've pushed the leading edge without pulling the trailing edge forward. The result is a landscape where yesterday's cutting edge is today's legacy, and the "modern" stack is already fragmented under the weight of new demands.

The evolution is easy enough to trace. Data warehouses gave us structured, governed reporting. Data lakes promised to store everything, structured or not, for future use. Lakehouse approaches tried to blend the discipline of warehouses with the flexibility of lakes. Data mesh and data fabric emerged to decentralize, democratize, and connect analytics across domains.

Now, AI adoption is accelerating yet another shift—toward vector databases, semantic layers, and specialized AI pipelines.

But through all these shifts, old platforms rarely disappear. We keep the warehouse because finance still depends on it. We keep the lake because data science still dips into it. We bolt on the lakehouse for hybrid workloads, and we spin up mesh nodes for domain-specific ownership. The result: a patchwork of analytical environments that don't fully align—each with its own governance model, data definitions, and integration quirks.

Managing Analytical Data

Analytical data management should be intentional. That may sound obvious, but too often we treat it as a by-product of the technology stack, not as a discipline in its own right. We continue to add platforms, ingest more sources, and experiment with new architectures—without verifying whether the entire landscape still serves business purposes and meets today's needs.

Over the past three decades, the platforms have frequently shifted. We started with tightly structured enterprise data warehouses. Then came data lakes, promising cheap, unlimited storage for all data types. Lakehouse architectures emerged to blend warehouse discipline with lake flexibility. Data mesh and data fabric concepts followed, pushing for distributed ownership and connectivity.

Now, AI adoption is driving yet another layer of change—vector databases, semantic layers, and specialized ML pipelines.

I see five recurring challenges in nearly every analytics environment. They're not new, but they're stubborn: platform sprawl, analytical silos, metric disparity, tool friction, and legacy gravity.

Platform Sprawl: Every Architecture Stays in Play

Platform sprawl is the analytical counterpart to operational data sprawl. We now have data warehouses, data lakes, lakehouses, mesh domains, and AI-ready stores—often running side-by-side in the same organization. Each has its own ingestion, storage, and query layers; its own governance model; its own cost footprint.

We rarely decommission the old when adopting the new. That's why the warehouse, the lake, and the lakehouse often all hold overlapping data. We replicate datasets between them, transform them differently in each, and sometimes can't remember which copy is most accurate or most recent.

The result isn't just expensive—it's confusing. Different teams pull the same data from different platforms and arrive at different answers. Over time, platform sprawl turns the analytical environment into a tangle of competing "sources of truth" that are difficult to reconcile and even harder to trust.

Analytical Silos: Isolated Islands of Insight

Analytical silos form when specific business units, domains, or projects build analytical environments for their own purposes—often with their own tools, models, and definitions.

In a mesh or domain-driven world, some degree of autonomy is the point. But without strong coordination, silos mean the marketing dashboard and the finance cube each track "revenue" differently, and neither reconciles perfectly with the warehouse.

Silos also tend to duplicate effort. One group might build a customer segmentation model without realizing that another group already has one—just using different attributes, algorithms, and datasets. The result: parallel work streams producing similar insights that don't line up, and with no clear way to decide which is "right."

Metric Disparity: When the Same Measure Means Different Things

Metric disparity is the analytical equivalent of operational data disparity. It occurs when the same metric, such as customer count, revenue, or churn, means different things in different analytical systems. Sometimes the differences are subtle: timing of recognition, rules for inclusion and exclusion of data, or rounding conventions. Other times, they're fundamental: entirely different definitions of what is being measured.

The warehouse might define "new customer" based on closed deals. The self-service BI layer might define it based on the first purchase date. The AI model might use the registration date. Each is valid in its own context but they are incompatible in aggregate.

This disparity erodes trust in analytics. Meetings become debates over definitions rather than discussions of action. People start pulling only from "their" system because it gives the numbers they expect.

> *Once trust is lost, analytics loses its value as a decision-making tool.*

Tool Friction: When Analytics Gets in its Own Way

Analytical friction happens when the effort to locate, reconcile, and use data outweighs the value of the insights. Tool friction is a major driver—different teams using different BI tools, query engines, transformation frameworks, or semantic layers that don't align.

Analysts often spend more time finding and cleaning the right data than actually analyzing it. They deal with mismatched column names, conflicting metadata, and incompatible data types between tools. By the time the data is ready, the original question may have shifted—or the decision window may have closed.

In high-velocity business environments, delay means lost opportunities. In slower-moving contexts, it wastes resources and frustrates users. In both cases, friction makes it easy to fall back on gut instinct or personal spreadsheets—diminishing the contributions and value of analytical systems.

Legacy Gravity: The Pull Keeping Old Systems in Orbit

Legacy gravity is what happens when older platforms and models remain embedded in processes long after their technology moment has passed. They can't be shut down because too many reports, integrations, or executive dashboards still depend on them.

The finance department still runs month-end reporting from the old warehouse. Certain compliance processes still rely on ETL scripts written a decade ago. That legacy code may be brittle, but rewriting it is risky and expensive—so it stays.

Meanwhile, analytical teams are asked to deliver cutting-edge AI insights while keeping these legacy systems alive. The old drags on the new, slowing adoption of modern practices and splitting attention between innovation and maintenance.

Analytical Data Chaos: The Compounding Effect

When platform sprawl, analytical silos, metric disparity, tool friction, and legacy gravity intersect, the result is analytical data chaos. It's the condition where the same business question can yield multiple, equally "correct" answers depending on which platform you query, which metric definition you use, and which copy of the data you trust.

Analytical chaos may not halt day-to-day business operations the way operational chaos can. Still, it undermines strategic decision-making, erodes trust in data-driven processes, and diminishes the return on decades of investment in analytical systems.

The fix isn't just about adopting the next big architecture or a shiny new tool. It's aligning what we already have, retiring what no longer serves, and governing definitions, models, and flows so that insight remains consistent—no matter how fast technology changes.

FOUR

An Architectural View of Data Management

Data sprawl. Data silos. Data disparity. Data friction.

These are not abstract ideas—they are the everyday realities of today's operational and analytical systems. They shape how data is created, stored, moved, and interpreted. And they aren't going away on their own. To achieve meaningful progress in data management, we must take deliberate action. That begins by asking a hard but essential question: What should we do about it? The answer lies in rethinking the architecture that shapes how data—both operational and analytical—is created, shared, and used.

In many organizations, the current data management architecture wasn't so much designed as it was assembled over time. For operational data management, systems were added, interfaces were built, one application was connected to another...then another...and another. Integration happened out of necessity, not strategy. What we're left with is a patchwork of data silos, point-to-point data feeds, and brittle dependencies—all treated as normal because that's how transactional systems have always been handled.

For analytical data, we've made more deliberate architectural moves—data warehouses, data lakes, lakehouses, master data hubs, and more recently, data mesh domains. These platforms were meant to unify and standardize data for reporting, analytics, and now AI. Yet, they too have become a layered landscape where older platforms are rarely retired, definitions drift, and data is copied endlessly between systems.

What's striking is how closely the challenges on each side mirror one another.

Operational Data Challenge	Analytical Data Challenge	Shared Impact
Data Sprawl — uncontrolled growth of sources, systems, and formats.	**Platform Sprawl —** accumulation of warehouses, lakes, lakehouses, mesh nodes, and AI stores.	Multiple environments to manage, each with its own tools, standards, governance, and costs.
Data Silos — isolated data tied to specific systems or departments.	**Analytical Silos —** domain- or project-specific analytics with differing tools and models.	Fragmented views of the business; difficulty in creating a single, trusted version of the truth.
Data Disparity — inconsistent structures, semantics, and quality for the same concepts.	**Metric Disparity —** conflicting definitions, inclusion/exclusion rules, and calculations.	Loss of trust, endless reconciliation, and inconsistent decision-making.

Operational Data Challenge	Analytical Data Challenge	Shared Impact
Data Friction — difficulty moving or using data due to inconsistencies or unclear definitions.	**Tool Friction —** inefficiencies caused by incompatible BI tools, semantic layers, or query engines.	More time is spent finding, cleaning, and reconciling data than analyzing it.
Global Data — complexity from geography, regulation, and localization.	**Legacy Gravity —** persistent reliance on outdated analytical systems and models.	Increased maintenance burden, slower modernization, and higher risk in change.

Table 1: Parallels in Operational and Analytical Data Challenges.

Why Architecture Matters Now

Operationally, the data scope continues to expand. With the rapid growth of IoT devices, automation platforms, and smart systems, the instinct has been to keep doing what we've done before: stitch the systems together with custom-crafted data flows. But this method doesn't scale. It doesn't simplify. It amplifies the very problems we're trying to solve—creating even more silos, more isolated data pipelines, and more complexity.

Analytically, AI adoption is accelerating change—pushing organizations to add vector databases, semantic layers, and ML pipelines on top of an already crowded platform ecosystem. Without coordinated architectural thinking, these additions may create more fragmentation than capability.

The lesson is clear: we need to have a single, cohesive data management architecture—not separate operational and analytical architectures. Operational data chaos undermines analytical reliability; analytical inconsistency feeds back into operational decisions. A coherent architecture must span both worlds.

Rethinking Data Management Architecture

Today's typical data management architecture is based on some fundamental assumptions that need to change. First, assuming that point-to-point interfaces are a feasible solution for the sharing of operational data. And second, that data copies and data integration are sufficient to meet analytical data requirements. We need to challenge these assumptions. We need to do it differently.

> *It is time to rethink data management architecture. The call for rethinking isn't just about replacing the old with the new. It's about how architecture can help bring coherence to operational data. It's about reducing complexity, aligning meaning, and building systems that are easier to manage, more resilient to change, and designed to work together.*

The goal is a connected, resilient, and manageable data ecosystem—one that makes both operational and analytical processes trustworthy, consistent, and actionable. We need an approach to data management architecture that balances innovation with retirement of old technologies, and that prevents legacy systems and practices from becoming barriers to new capabilities and to business and data management agility. We've reached the point where patchwork fixes won't work. It is time to rethink data management architecture—not just for operational systems or for analytics, but for the entire data landscape.

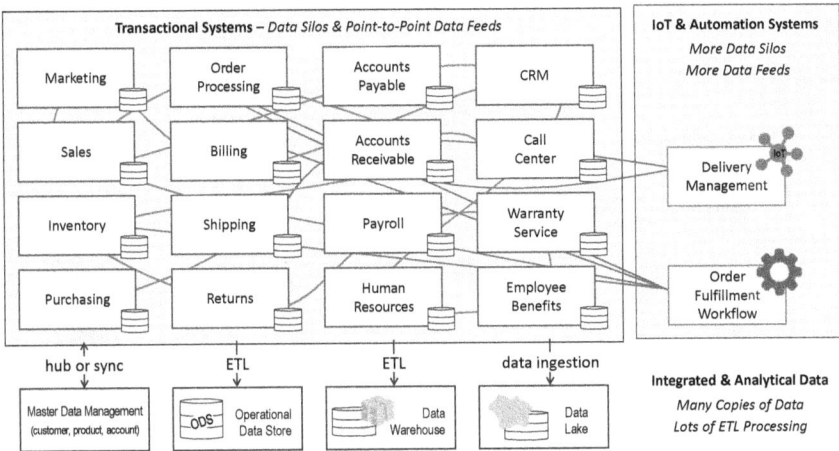

Figure 7: Typical Data Management Architecture.

Modernizing and Unifying Data Management Architecture

Architecture is about structure. It's about bringing order and intentionality to systems that are otherwise fragmented, reactive, and difficult to manage. When we talk about rethinking data management architecture, we're talking about moving beyond traditional patterns that have failed to scale—and establishing a new foundation that supports interoperability, clarity, and sustainable growth.

There are three core concepts at the center of this rethinking: domain data management, data semantics, and data products. Each one addresses a fundamental weakness in legacy data architecture. Together, they form the basis for a modern, adaptable, and well-structured approach to operational data management.

Domain Data Management

Domain data management is a fundamental shift that decentralizes authority and responsibility for managing data. Rather than relying on a single, centralized data management team to control all aspects of data definition, quality, integration, and stewardship, a domain-oriented architecture distributes those responsibilities across multiple data management domains.

Domains are typically source-aligned—structured around where data originates. And data origins naturally map to functional areas of the business. For example, domains may be aligned with sales, orders, inventory, financials, human resources, and service. Each domain owns and manages the data it produces. Each domain is accountable for the quality, clarity, and accessibility of its data. And collectively, these domains take responsibility for the larger operational data ecosystem.

In this model, the architecture aligns with the business. The systems that create data and the teams that understand its meaning are also the stewards of that data. Coordination remains essential, but responsibility is distributed—and that distribution is a powerful step toward reducing bottlenecks, clarifying accountability, and improving data quality at the source.

Data Semantics

Data semantics uses an enterprise semantic model to bring consistency to meaning across diverse and often incompatible data sources. A semantic layer, built on a clear and well-defined semantic foundation, enables the practical mapping of local data dialects to a common data language. Sales data may be expressed one way, service data another, and financial data yet another. But with a semantic framework in place, each dialect can be interpreted, translated, and aligned.

This is the essence of data interoperability. Instead of building custom logic for every pair of systems—and every pair of definitions—we define shared meaning once, then map to it. Local systems continue to speak in their own terms, but the architecture provides a common language to support system-to-system communication and data sharing. Replacing point-to-point feeds with semantic translation reduces complexity, increases resilience, and enables a sustainable model to break down data silos.

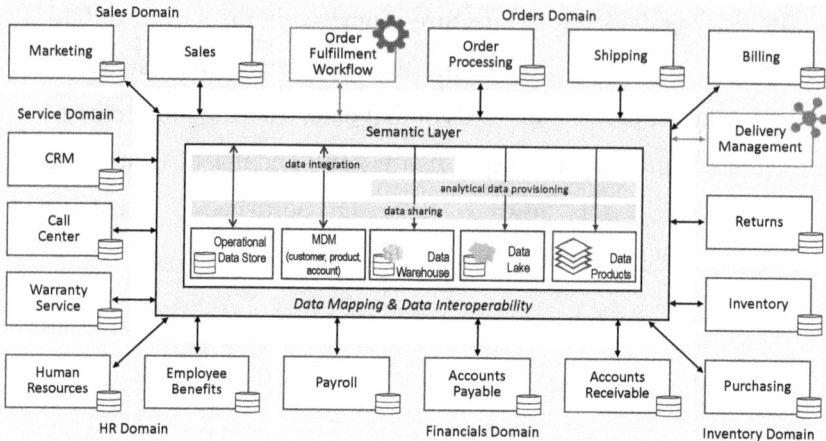

Figure 8: Rethinking Architecture: Domains, Semantics, and Products.

Data Products

Data products are consumer-ready, purpose-specific collections of data that are built for accessibility, usability, and reuse. A data product is more than just a dataset. It is a managed, packaged offering of data functionality, designed to serve a clearly defined need. Well-constructed data products are:

- Reusable across multiple consumers and use cases
- Scalable across data volumes and environments
- Functionally precise, tailored to support specific business or analytical processes

Data products benefit from the semantic layer. With semantics-based metadata and APIs, data products become a clean, consistent, and highly effective way to integrate and share data.

They offer a modern alternative to ad hoc queries, unmanaged extracts, or complex, monolithic data pipelines.

Data products also simplify provisioning for analytics. Semantic queries allow consumers to request data in terms they understand. Semantics-based schemas enable clarity and alignment across systems. And the same mappings that support interoperability also serve to define transformations for master data reconciliation, ODS integration, and data warehouse loading.

In this architectural view, semantics and domain alignment are not theoretical ideas—they are data interoperability mechanisms. They define how data is structured, shared, and understood. When applied through data products, they make those structures consumable, dependable, and scalable. When applied to data sharing and analytical data provisioning, they support the necessary balance that sustains the value of data warehouses, data lakes, master data hubs, etc., while removing dependency on these data resources to deliver future capabilities.

Next Generation Data Architecture

Rethinking data management architecture is about more than modernizing. It's about *unifying* operational and analytical ecosystems so they work as one. It's about *simplifying* overly complex integration patterns and *aligning* definitions so that the meaning is consistent everywhere. It's about *streamlining* processes to remove bottlenecks, *standardizing* models and governance, and *integrating* capabilities across domains.

We are *optimizing* for performance, cost, and agility while *harmonizing* differences between systems. We are *connecting* data across business functions, *balancing* the needs of legacy and modern platforms, and *scaling* without creating new silos. We are *securing* our data through embedded compliance and *future-proofing* the architecture to adapt to inevitable technology shifts.

This isn't a one-time upgrade—it's a fundamental shift toward an architecture that is resilient, interoperable, and designed for sustainable growth. Done right, it replaces fragmentation with coherence, redundancy with efficiency, and chaos with clarity—across the entire data landscape.

FIVE

Data Interoperability Benefits and Barriers

To understand what data interoperability is, we'll begin with some basic definitions. First, we'll look at the concept of interoperability, without limiting it to data. Wikipedia defines interoperability as "a characteristic of a product or system to work with other products or systems. Types of interoperability include syntactic interoperability, where two systems can communicate with each other, and cross-domain interoperability, where multiple organizations work together to exchange information."[1] In short, systems or components can communicate, and this communication produces meaningful and functional cooperation.

---

[1] https://en.wikipedia.org/wiki/Interoperability.

The two forms of interoperability described—syntactic interoperability and cross-domain interoperability—map directly to the architectural concepts introduced earlier: data semantics and domain data management. Together, they form the foundation for transitioning from disconnected systems to coherent, interoperable data environments.

We've been working with the concepts of software interoperability for decades. It's the idea that systems—built by different teams, using different platforms—can still interchange interpretable information. They do this by adhering to well-defined communication protocols, standardized data formats, and shared rules for interaction. REST APIs, messaging protocols, service contracts—these are all familiar tools of software interoperability.

What's new is the idea of applying these principles to the data itself—independent of any specific software or application. That's the shift. We move from systems that work together to data that works together—across platforms, across vendors, and across business domains.

> *Data interoperability is defined as the ability of systems and services that create, exchange, and consume data to have clear, shared expectations for the contents, context, and meaning of that data.*

Systems and services still matter, but interoperability happens at the data level—and specifically, at the level of metadata that describes what the data is, what it means, and how it should be understood.

That's the role of data semantics. With a well-defined semantic layer, data products and systems can interact much like software components—sending, receiving, and interpreting information in ways that are consistent and predictable. But unlike software interoperability, where protocols define the structure of communication, data interoperability depends on meaning. It's about making sure data stored in different formats, models, or locations can be understood and used together, without ambiguity or translation errors. Achieving that depends on one critical factor: a standardized language for shared understanding.

In data interoperability, this shared language is provided by data semantics—the framework that defines not only the structure of data but also its meaning. Semantics allows us to move beyond structural connections and into semantic connections—where the purpose and interpretation of the data is understood across domains and use cases.

Data Interoperability versus Data Integration

It is helpful to understand the distinctions between data integration and data interoperability—to compare them, recognize their similarities, and appreciate their differences. The two concepts are closely related (and may be used together) but they are not the same.

Analytical data integration is almost exclusively based on copying and transforming data. ETL and similar processes acquire data from sources, transform it to conform to a standard schema, and load the transformed data into curated data stores such as data warehouses and data lakes. With this make-a-copy approach:

- The target schema defines data equivalence. For example, customer data from order processing, customer service, and sales is merged by resolving content, structure, encoding, and semantic differences—all to conform to a single, prescribed definition of "customer" as defined in a data warehouse, ODS, or another repository schema.

- Data translations are built into ETL processing. Business rules and mappings are implemented as transformation logic.

- Integrated data is stored as copies of the original data with transformations applied.

- Data lineage becomes a question. Where did this copy come from? How has it been transformed or modified?

- Source schema and encoding changes are disruptive. ETL processes must be updated. The downstream ODS or warehouse schema may need to change. Reporting and analytics errors may occur.

- Each change introduces disruption, and disruption is a clear sign of technical debt.

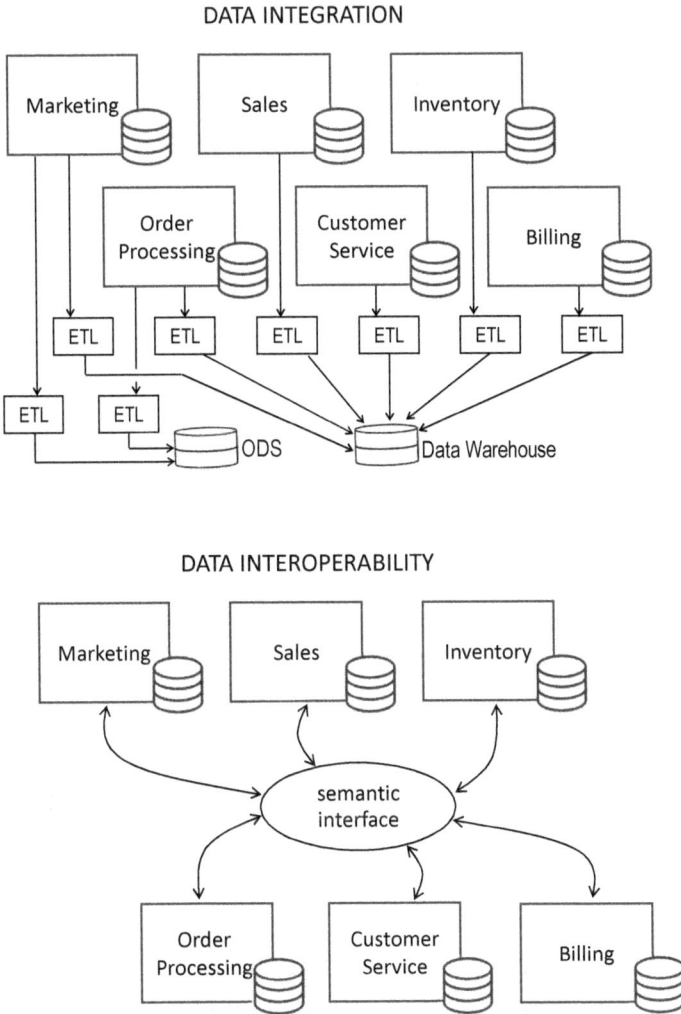

DATA INTEGRATION

DATA INTEROPERABILITY

Figure 9: Data Integration versus Data Interoperability.

Data interoperability offers a fundamentally different approach. The interoperability model connects systems through a semantic interface. Instead of extracting and transforming data into a common repository, systems communicate directly, using shared semantics to interpret data consistently across systems. With data interoperability:

- Data equivalence is defined by a semantic layer that serves as a common language understood by all participating systems.

- Translations, if needed, are local. Each system is responsible for interpreting incoming data in terms it understands. For example, when sales receives customer data from customer service, the data is expressed in shared semantic terms, and sales applies local translation as needed—converting from the common language to its own dialect.

- Data copies are minimized. The emphasis shifts from replication to communication—from storing data centrally to sharing it meaningfully.

- Schema and encoding changes are localized. Changes to one system's structure or logic stay within that system's boundary, reducing ripple effects across the architecture.

- Technical debt is reduced. With fewer centralized transformations and no need to retrofit every schema change into a global model, the architecture becomes more resilient and adaptable.

> *Integration and interoperability are not mutually exclusive. They can and should coexist. It is not desirable or practical to replace all data integration with data interoperability. Good data management architecture should accommodate both.*

Data interoperability is an alternative to data integration—not a replacement for it. Interoperability is a very effective way for data systems to talk to other data systems. A semantic interface can replace all of the point-to-point data feeds between operational systems. But that doesn't eliminate the need for data warehouses, operational data stores, or master data repositories. Data integration is here for the long term. Data interoperability is an additional capability to be added to data architecture and to the data management toolbox.

Why Data Interoperability?

> *Interoperability combats sprawl.*

Sprawl is one compelling reason to add data interoperability to your data management toolbox—not just data sprawl, but operational system sprawl. In most organizations today, the number of operational systems continues to grow. It's not just more systems; it's more types of systems, from more sources, with more variation in how data is managed. A simple example illustrates the point:

Imagine an operational environment with just ten systems: Four are SaaS applications—CRM, Marketing, Sales, and Call Center—each from a different vendor, and clearly not integrated with one another. Four more—Order Processing, Shipping, Billing, and Accounts Receivable—are ERP systems, but two different ERP platforms, with integration gaps between them. The remaining two systems—Inventory and Purchasing—are legacy custom applications. These may be loosely connected to one another but are not natively integrated with sales, order processing, or billing.

This example is modest compared to the complexity found in large enterprises. Yet even in this small portfolio, the integration challenges are clear:

- Different system types (SaaS, ERP, legacy, custom)
- Different vendors, each with its own platform and data model
- Inconsistent data definitions, formats, and encoding methods
- Overlapping data maintained across multiple systems—often redundantly and inconsistently
- Isolated data silos, with no shared understanding of semantics or structure

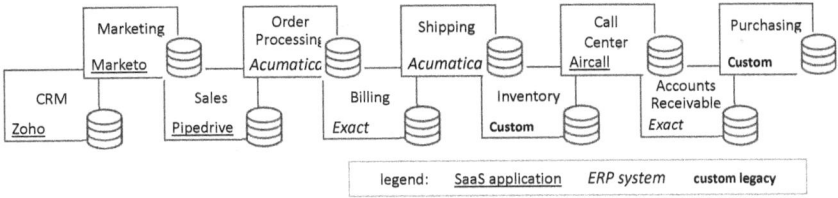

Figure 10: Operational Systems SprawlOperational Systems Sprawl.

The outcome is familiar: a patchwork of point-to-point data flows—brittle, complex, and difficult to maintain. Application-to-application communication relies on custom-coded interfaces, hardwired transformations, and one-off solutions that don't scale. As systems multiply and diversify, this architecture becomes harder to manage and slower to change. New systems are difficult to onboard. Changes to existing systems create downstream ripple effects. And the effort required to reconcile, reformat, and interpret data only grows.

Data interoperability is a practical solution. Instead of treating each integration as a custom effort, interoperability creates a shared foundation. This semantic interface allows systems to exchange data in ways that are meaningful, consistent, and resilient to change. In a sprawl environment, where systems are decentralized, platforms vary widely, and redundancy and inconsistency are the norm, data interoperability brings structure, clarity, and a scalable model for data communication.

Interoperability simplifies system-to-system communications.

Continuing the example of ten operational systems, many different communications occur.

- Sales tells order processing to fulfill an order
- Order processing tells billing what amount to bill
- Order processing asks accounts receivable about the status of a customer account
- Sales asks CRM about upsell opportunities
- Marketing asks CRM for customer profiles
- And many more app-to-app communications

This is what those problematic point-to-point data feeds are all about.

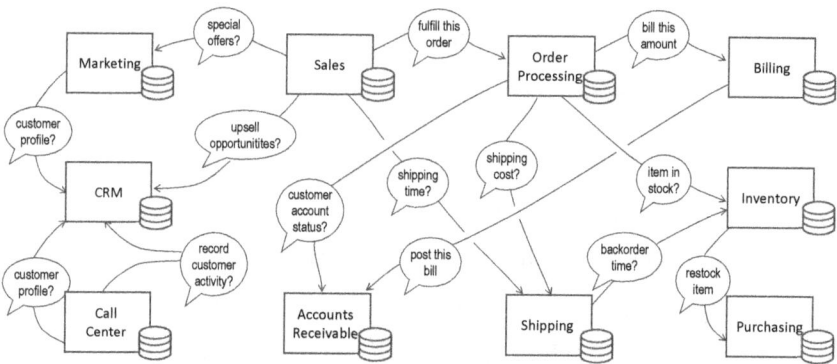

Figure 11: Systems Communicate With Data.

A closer look at how these communications are implemented reveals just how complex point-to-point integration can become. What appears to be a simple interaction between two systems is often two separate data flows—one for the request and one for the response. That means two connections to manage, two opportunities for failure, and two custom implementations to maintain. And those data flows take many different technical forms:

- Process-to-process batch transfers, scheduled and time-sensitive
- Process-to-database batch updates, often tied to overnight jobs
- Real-time process-to-database exchanges, tightly coupled and error-prone
- Application-to-application real-time interactions, implemented via APIs and often vendor-specific

Each form has its own logic, timing, error-handling, and monitoring requirements. Multiply that by dozens—or even hundreds—of application connections, and the operational overhead becomes enormous.

Interoperability provides scalability.

This example shows a relatively small number of things—fourteen communication needs among ten systems. In reality, there are many more system-to-system communications than the 14 shown as examples. The applications and the business processes that they support are closely interconnected. Beyond the initial examples, there is a need for communication between sales and accounts receivable, sales and call center, sales and inventory, billing and call center, inventory and shipping, shipping and call center, and potentially many others. It quickly becomes apparent that with each new communication need, the tangled mess of app-to-app data flows becomes increasingly complex and difficult to manage. And it gets even more messy when we recognize that there are many more than the ten systems supporting business operations. More communications. More data flows. Lots of stuff going on. And this is how we get to that thing called data chaos.

Instead of building unique connections for every pair of systems, interoperability introduces a shared semantic interface—a common foundation that each system uses to send and receive data. The result is a scalable architecture where:

- New systems don't require new connections to every existing system
- Communications are standardized and easier to monitor, trace, and manage
- The architecture grows in capability without growing in fragility

Interoperability scales. Point-to-point does not.

Interoperability reduces complexity.

The most common way for operational systems to communicate is through point-to-point connections—a collection of single-purpose data flows, each crafted for a specific integration need. It's the default model in many organizations, and it has been in place for decades. But familiarity should not be mistaken for effectiveness.

Point-to-point is not only complex, it is complicated. Each data flow is independently built and managed. There's no central pattern, no shared framework, no architectural structure that connects the dots. The result is disorganized and confusing. It is a patchwork of isolated data flows that grows harder to manage with each new system or communication requirement.

From an architectural perspective, the challenge is visibility. A big-picture view is difficult to assemble. There is no clear map. There is no simple way to compare or analyze the collection of data flows—to understand where they overlap, where they differ, or where they might conflict. Even fundamental questions become difficult to answer:

- What business information is being exchanged? What specific data is flowing?
- Which communications are two-way?
- Which are batch, and how frequently do they run?
- Which are real-time, and how are they triggered?
- When and where do systems use databases as intermediaries for data exchange?
- How are errors detected, logged, and resolved?
- What happens when a schema or data structure changes?
- What systems or processes must be retested when something changes?

This is the core of the problem. The point-to-point approach may seem manageable at a small scale, but as systems and integration needs grow, it doesn't just become more complex—it becomes intensely convoluted.

It is difficult to manage. It is fragile when change occurs. It is expensive to extend. And it creates an environment where every new requirement adds more risk and more cost. Point-to-point integration doesn't scale. It obscures structure and increases chaos. That is the reason why data interoperability is more than just a different approach—it's a necessary evolution in how we approach system-to-system communication.

Interoperability is a natural fit for master data.

Master data management (MDM) is a good use case for data interoperability. At its core, MDM is a system for integrating operational data. But too often, there's a tendency to treat master data as if it were analytical—something created for reports or dashboards. That view is flawed.

Master data is operational. Every instance of customer, product, account, employee, location, or any other core entity originates in operational systems and processes—not in data warehouses, data lakes, or other analytical platforms. Master data may be used in analytics, but it is created and maintained by operational systems.

The MDM challenge lies in reconciling the differences across operational systems in a way that does not disrupt local data management. Ideally, each system continues to function with its own terminology, definitions, and encoding practices.

Interoperability makes that possible by mapping local characteristics to a shared semantic model. That semantic model serves as a common language—a shared understanding of master data that all systems can connect to. Systems operate locally with their own terms.

- Semantic mapping links local views to standard terms.
- Data can be shared across systems through semantics-based translation.
- Enterprise consistency is established, while local system autonomy is maintained.

This approach enables an enterprise view of master data without requiring systems to conform to a single definition or structure. And this applies regardless of MDM architecture. Whether using a repository, a hub, a services model, or a synchronization pattern, semantics plays a supporting role, enhancing communication, alignment, and consistency across systems.

Data semantics improves master data management by making it easier to interpret, align, and share master data across a diverse and often disconnected portfolio of operational systems.

Interoperability supports analytics.

While much of the discussion around data interoperability and data semantics has focused on operational data, the same concepts and techniques also offer real, practical benefits for analytical data management.

Start with the enterprise data warehouse. Yes, it is integration-oriented, built on processes like ETL and ELT, but those processes can be greatly simplified and improved by incorporating data semantics. Think about the variety of data sources that contribute to a data warehouse: transactional systems, master data repositories, reference datasets, departmental marts, and external data feeds.

When those sources are semantically modeled and mapped, integration becomes far more purposeful. Data equivalence is determined by the semantic model, not just by structural alignment. The warehouse schema is based on agreed-upon business meaning, rather than local variations. Data transformations are driven by semantic mappings, which increase accuracy and reduce ambiguity. Lineage is easier to trace because the semantic layer captures both structure and meaning. And most importantly, the work of integration is reduced—less manual coding, fewer one-off transformations, and a more sustainable path forward.

Now consider the data lake—often touted for flexibility, but also infamous for becoming a data swamp. Data semantics brings order to chaos. With clearly defined enterprise terms and meanings, AI and machine learning can be used to automatically tag incoming data streams. An ingestion process can recognize and classify data as customer data, transaction data, product data, or revenue data—and apply semantic tags accordingly. Auto-tagging enriches metadata. It improves searchability, discoverability, and organization. It's one of the key differences between a data lake that delivers value—and one that just stores data.

Then there's the analytical data pipeline—the process of assembling, shaping, and preparing data for models, visualizations, and insights. When data is requested in semantic terms, the semantic layer can orchestrate the composition process, selecting the right data from the right sources—warehouse, lake, or elsewhere—and minimizing unnecessary processing. Instead of reengineering data transformations for every analytic use case, the semantic layer handles the interpretation. Instead of hardwiring pipelines to specific source schemas, semantic queries retrieve what's needed in the business context, enabling downstream analytics to proceed in the analytic context.

In this way, data interoperability, powered by semantics, bridges the gap between operational systems and analytical platforms. It doesn't replace data integration. But it enhances it, simplifies it, and creates a stronger foundation for delivering consistent, meaningful data to the people and processes that need it most.

Architectural Barriers to Interoperability

Data interoperability begins with data management architecture. The first step in moving toward interoperability is to acknowledge current architectural bias, recognizing the things we do when designing and applying architecture, as well as the things we need to do to make interoperability a reality. All mainstream architectures—data warehousing, data lake, data lakehouse, and data mesh—have inherent biases that should be acknowledged.

- **Bias 1—Operational versus Analytical Data.** The first area of bias lies in the treatment of operational versus analytical data. Most architectures focus on analytical data, treating operational data only as a source— something to be extracted, transformed, and loaded into analytic platforms. But operational data has value beyond its role in analytics. It supports core business operations, facilitates real-time decisions, and underpins master data domains. Effective architecture must treat operational data as a first-class asset, with the same level of care, structure, and planning as analytical data.

- **Bias 2—Integration as the Only Option.** Integration is often assumed to be the sole method to resolve data disparity and break down data silos. A balanced approach uses both integration and interoperability, recognizing that some scenarios are best served by transforming and loading data, while others benefit from mapping and translating through shared semantics. Good architecture should make room for both options, based on fitness for purpose.

- **Bias 3—Overuse of Data Copies.** The third bias is the overuse of data copies. Data gets replicated—from operational systems to data warehouses, from warehouses to data marts, from transactional stores to master data hubs, and across zones of data lakes. In many cases, proliferation of data copies is not the result of a deliberate architectural choice, but rather a default behavior. Copying data to configure it for each use case is common practice, but not without cost. Replication increases storage requirements, complicates data protection and governance, and introduces risks of inconsistency. Interoperability offers an alternative—a way to provide data functionality without excessive copying.

- **Bias 4—Rigid Schemas.** The fourth bias is shaped by how data use is interpreted through rigid, purpose-built schemas. Much of analytic data infrastructure—data warehouses, marts, curated data zones, etc.—is designed with fixed structure and specific use cases in mind. As a result, analytic practices are often adapted to fit the shape of the available data, rather than designing data to meet evolving analytic needs. This rigidity can distort intent and obscure business value. A good alternative composes data to serve individual use cases—assembling fit-for-purpose datasets using modern engineering practices. That approach aligns well with semantic data layers and data products, enabling greater agility while preserving consistency.

Addressing these architectural barriers begins with awareness. Architectural choices made in the past have led to siloed, fragmented, and duplicative data environments. Moving toward interoperability means questioning the defaults, exploring alternatives, and designing with shared semantics and purposeful structure in mind.

Common analytical data management architectures—data warehousing, data lake, data lakehouse, data mesh—are geared toward data integration, data consolidation, or both. None of them are designed for data interoperability. That doesn't mean that these are *bad* approaches. There is, in fact, a lot of good in them. We need the ability to consolidate data, and we need data integration capabilities. The goal is not to replace these architectures, but to extend them because we also need data interoperability. To extend them, we need to understand the barriers to interoperability inherent in each of them:

- **Data warehousing** centralizes integrated data for reporting and analytics using ETL/ELT processes and fixed schemas. Variants include hub architectures, with a centralized enterprise data warehouse as the authoritative source, and bus architectures, with modular marts sharing conformed dimensions. While proven effective for data integration, this pattern inhibits interoperability in three ways. Multiple copies of data increase redundancy and inconsistency. Rigid schemas limit flexibility. Integration as the default method disregards opportunities for semantic access.

- **Data lakes** provide centralized repositories for storing large volumes of structured, semi-structured, and unstructured data in its native format. They organize content into zones—raw, refined, and curated— reflecting stages of readiness. Data lakes support schema-on-read, which enables flexible use for analytics, data science, and machine learning. However, loose structure in raw zones prevents immediate interoperability. The absence of standard semantics across datasets hinders system-to-system sharing without transformation. Refined and curated zones often repeat integration's copy-related problems, introducing redundancy and potential inconsistency.

- **Data lakehouse** architecture combines the flexibility of a data lake with the schema enforcement of a warehouse, often through a delta lake layer that supports SQL queries and ACID transactions. This hybrid aims to deliver the best of both worlds but inherits the drawbacks of each. From the data lake side, it retains the proliferation of data copies and integration-based curation. From the data warehouse side, it imposes rigid schemas that can force use cases to adapt to the data, while still favoring integration over interoperability.

- **Data mesh** distributes data management across domains, each owning and governing its data within enterprise and federated governance constraints. Domains publish data products, ideally using shared infrastructure, to support other domains and analytical needs. While interoperability is addressed through product standards, these standards often focus on APIs rather than shared semantics. As a result, semantic alignment—the foundation of true interoperability—remains incomplete. The data mesh is moving in the right direction, introducing domain data management and data products, but it does not yet fully address the semantic dimension.

While each mainstream data architecture has proven strengths, none are inherently designed for interoperability. Their current forms lean heavily toward integration and carry the biases of data copies, schema rigidity, and limited recognition of the value of operational data. These limitations, however, do not mean we should discard what works or start again with yet another architectural pattern.

The path forward is to extend these architectures, not to replace them. By introducing a semantic layer into each, we can enable systems to communicate through shared meaning while preserving existing capabilities. In a warehouse, semantics can reduce rigid coupling and streamline transformations. In a lake, it can bring order and discoverability. In a lakehouse, it can bridge flexible storage with meaningful structure. In a mesh, it can complete the vision of domain-based data sharing. That path begins by understanding the role of data semantics for data interoperability.

Six

Data Semantics and Data Interoperability

Semantics refers to what individual words mean and to what they mean when we put them together to form phrases and sentences. Data semantics is focused on how a data object represents a concept or object in the real world. It is about what data language means in terms of things in the real world, what the individual words mean, and also what they mean when we put them together—how they are related or how they interact.

One of the severe consequences of data silos and disparate data is uncertainty and confusion about what is meant by the words that label and describe data. Opportunities for ambiguity, inconsistency, and misinterpretation are abundant. In a retail business, for example, uncertainty might surface in many forms:

- What's the difference between a customer and a user?
- Is a return the same as a cancellation?

- When is an order considered fulfilled?
- What counts as a successful transaction?
- What's the difference between a promotion and a discount?
- Who qualifies as a loyal customer?
- What is the difference between a cart and a wishlist?
- Is store pickup considered a shipment?
- When is inventory considered available?
- What is a backorder, and how is it different from an out-of-stock item?
- What's the difference between gross sales and net sales?
- What constitutes a fraudulent transaction?
- When is a product considered defective versus damaged?
- What's the difference between product category and product type?

This is the nature of business terminology and data terminology. If we refer to a product as defective, we need to understand what it means. We need to know how it is similar to, and how it differs from, a damaged product. We have similar needs for pickup versus shipment and many other ambiguities.

The goal of data semantics is to establish standard terminology and assign a prescribed meaning to each standard term. Standard terms and prescribed meaning are necessary to get a common understanding of what things mean and to achieve unambiguous communication—communication without a high degree of uncertainty. This is the stuff that supports the three principles of data interoperability: shared context, shared content, and shared meaning.

The Role of Semantics in Data Management

Modeling data semantics captures and organizes the knowledge needed to create a semantic data layer. The semantic layer is the highest level of data abstraction. It is an abstract representation of data in business terms—the essential knowledge that enables mapping from obscure technical language to user-friendly language. By creating a standard and controlled vocabulary for naming and describing data, the semantic layer creates a business-friendly data access layer using the controlled vocabulary. Equally important, it creates a common view for data sharing. This is the key to resolving the inconsistencies and the data disparities that occur in data.

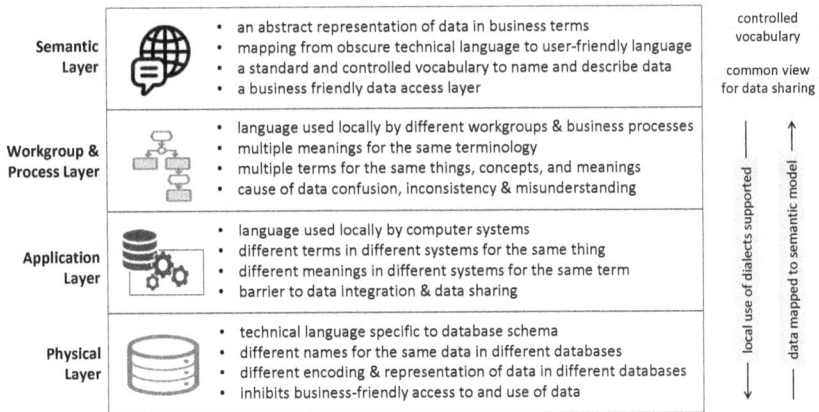

Figure 12: Four Layers of Data Abstraction.

At the next lower level of abstraction, with data semantics, we resolve the inconsistencies in language used locally by different work groups and business processes—the inconsistent language used by people and organizations. This is the work group and process layer where different work groups and different processes have multiple meanings for the same terminology and multiple terms for the same things. That results in confusion, inconsistency, misunderstanding, miscommunication, and misuse of data.

We can also resolve data disparities at the application level. In the application layer, we have language used locally by different computer systems, different terms in different systems for the same thing, different meanings for the same terms. And this makes data sharing, data integration, and data exchange exceptionally difficult.

And we can resolve inconsistencies at the physical level, where we have technical language that's specific to the database schema. Again, inconsistency in naming—different names for the same data in different databases, different ways of encoding and representing data in different databases. This gets in the way of business-friendly access to data and business-friendly use of data.

When the semantic layer is well-designed and applied, we can support the local dialects. With semantic mapping, it is not necessary that each workgroup, process, application, or database is changed to use standard terminology. Instead, we can map local

terminology to the semantic model—to the controlled vocabulary—
making it possible to translate between different data dialects.

The Semantic Layer and Data Interoperability

The challenge with local data dialects is data disparity at the work group process and application layers—many conflicts of context, content, and meaning across multiple layers, multiple organizations, and multiple systems. Disparity causes difficulties with data sharing and data exchange.

Data interoperability is a practical way to resolve those difficulties. It provides capabilities needed for application systems and databases to work together in a coordinated way, without requiring human intervention. We want to prevent data inconsistencies from hindering data sharing and effective communication among applications. Without a semantic layer, applications communicate with one another through point-to-point interfaces. One application feeds data to another application that requires the data. With lots of point-to-point data feeds, the result is a tangled mess of disorganized data feeds. Data translations are embedded in application code. Lots of application-to-application dependencies exist. This is complex and difficult, and it is custom coding for each interface. When changes occur, such as schema changes or changes in the ways that data is encoded, it takes a lot of investigation, analysis, and manual effort to determine the impact. And more effort to recode the interfaces so that they continue to work correctly. This approach builds in a very high level of technical debt.

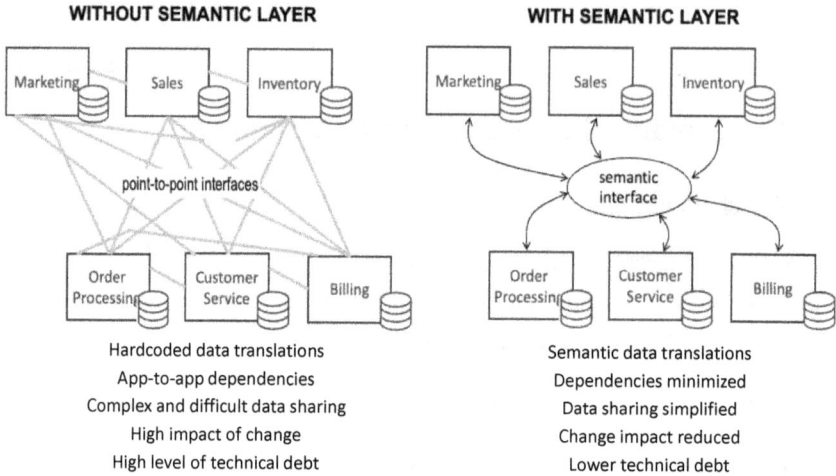

WITHOUT SEMANTIC LAYER	WITH SEMANTIC LAYER
Hardcoded data translations	Semantic data translations
App-to-app dependencies	Dependencies minimized
Complex and difficult data sharing	Data sharing simplified
High impact of change	Change impact reduced
High level of technical debt	Lower technical debt

Figure 13: Point-to-Point versus Semantic Interface.

Adding a semantic layer resolves many of these issues. Replacing point-to-point interfaces with a semantic interface uses common semantics (an agreed-upon standard vocabulary) to replace the code-based data translations. The semantic layer significantly reduces dependencies between applications. Data sharing is less complex. Schema and encoding changes are localized to the applications, eliminating the need to maintain and recode point-to-point interfaces. As a result, technical debt is substantially reduced.

SEVEN

Semantic Data Modeling

Semantic data modeling is a first step on the path to data interoperability. A semantic data model represents data in terms of named sets of objects, named relationships between objects, and named properties of objects and relationships. Naming is a key element of semantic data modeling, where model components are labeled with terms that constitute the standard vocabulary.

Semantic data modeling offers a structured approach to expressing the meaning of data. Semantic models are commonly expressed using graph models: knowledge graphs and property graphs. Graph modeling is a business-friendly, non-technical way to express semantics visually.

Knowledge Graphs

Knowledge graphs describe things and their relationships as triples: subject, predicate, object. Subjects and objects are things that are represented as nodes (labeled circles) in the graph. The predicate is a relationship, known as an edge in graph terminology, and represented as a labeled line. The edge uses an arrow to show direction—the path from subject to object.

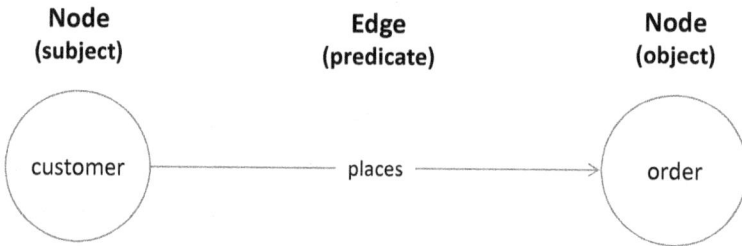

Node (subject)	Edge (predicate)	Node (object)

| customer | places ——————→ | order |

Figure 14: Triple Representation in a Graph Model.

This knowledge graph models a triple that can be expressed as a simple sentence: customer places order. This kind of modeling brings clarity to complex systems by breaking down real-world scenarios into understandable, sentence-like structures. It simplifies data relationships into visual and intuitive elements, making both meaning and connections easier to grasp and communicate.

Property Graphs

Property graphs extend the knowledge graph to include characteristics of nodes and edges. In graph terminology, the characteristics are known as properties. In the language of traditional entity-relationship modeling, nodes are the entities, predicates express relationships, and properties are attributes. In graph models, both entities and relationships have properties directly associated with them. This is different from entity-relationship models where properties of relationships are shown only when the relationship is modeled as an associative entity.

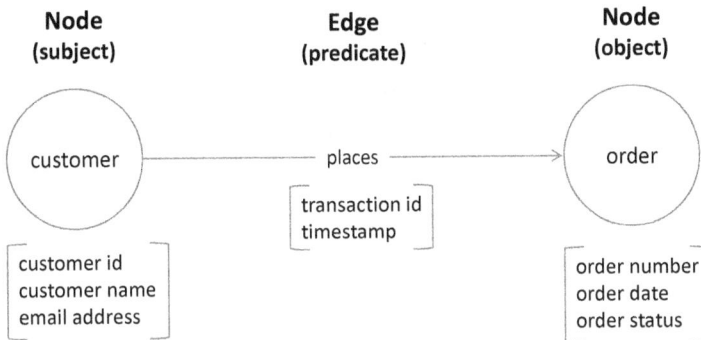

Figure 15: Properties in a Graph Model.

The Semantic Modeling Process

The process begins with scope setting to define the boundaries of semantic modeling projects. It is not realistic or practical to attempt to model everything at once. With scope setting, we ask what applications or business domains to model. We may be setting the scope for a single project or a series of multiple projects.

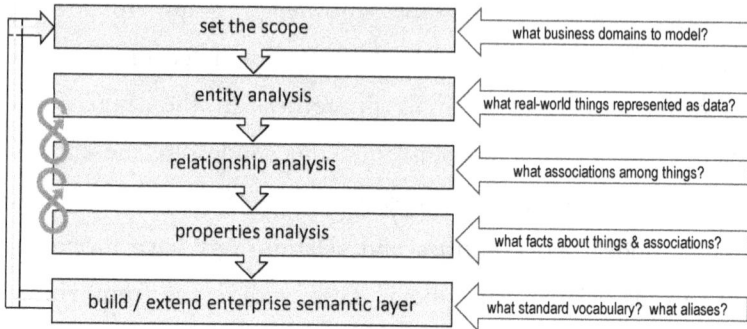

Figure 16: The Semantic Modeling Process.

With the scope determined, the heart of semantic modeling consists of entity analysis, relationship analysis, and properties analysis. Entity analysis identifies and names the things or entities represented as data—modeling nodes in the graph. Relationship analysis identifies and names the associations, connections, or interactions among things—the edges in the graph. Properties analysis identifies and names facts or attributes that describe things and associations.

In the diagram above, it looks like a linear process—entity analysis, followed by relationship analysis, followed by properties analysis. But in reality, it is not linear. In practice, you'll find that modeling only a few entities leads to discussion of and discovery of relationships. As you model relationships, you'll likely find and model additional entities. And the discussion of entities and relationships typically leads to the modeling of properties. Properties modeling, in turn, may lead to the discovery of more entities and relationships. So, it is really an iterative and nonlinear process—a simultaneous process of analyzing entities, relationships, and properties.

When modeling for an enterprise semantic layer, the goal is a single model representing the entire enterprise. In that case, only the first cycle of modeling—the first domain to be modeled— produces a new model. Each subsequent domain expands and extends the existing semantic model. This is a practical approach to building a single enterprise semantic data layer.

Perform entity analysis and relationship analysis together and iteratively to produce an ontology as a knowledge graph—a representation of things of interest with the relationships among those things expressed as triples.

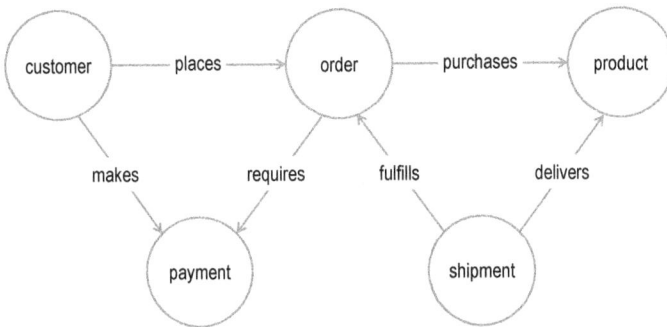

Figure 17: Ontology as a Knowledge Graph.

Entity Analysis

When analyzing the entities, ask what real-world things are or need to be represented as data. You can look at many sources to identify these things: subject matter expert (SME) knowledge, business forms and documents, reports, data sets, data models, and any other resources related to the modeling domain. Look for significant nouns that give names to a person, place, thing, concept, transaction, or event. Labeling persons as customers, for example, or places as locations. Be disciplined and selective about the labels that you use on the graph. Recognize synonyms, aliases, or other idiosyncrasies of language that may need to be acknowledged as local dialect. Model the things that you identify as nodes in a knowledge graph.

Relationship Analysis

To analyze relationships, examine the interconnections among things. The things of interest are those that are modeled as nodes in the graph—the things identified through entity analysis. Now we want to understand the relationships among those things. Again, look at all of the available knowledge sources—SME knowledge, business forms and documents, reports, data sets, data models, etc.—but now, instead of looking for nouns, look for verb forms that suggest actions taken. Work with the verb forms to find expressions that make sense as triples—customer places order, order purchases product, and so on—phrases that express active relationships. Model the relationships as edges and label them using active verb forms with directionality in mind—customer places order, not order placed by customer.

Terminology Analysis

Terminology analysis is an integral part of semantic modeling. Semantics describes how words are used and what they mean. So, terminology analysis is inherent in entity analysis, relationship analysis, and also properties analysis, which is yet to come. Terminology analysis establishes clarity and removes ambiguity about the labels given to nodes, edges, and properties on a graph.

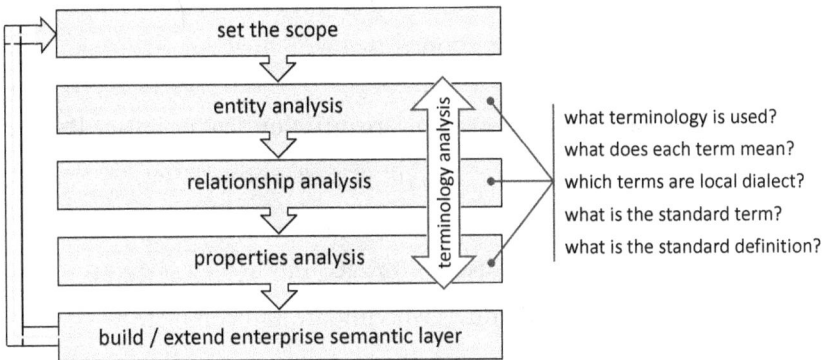

Figure 18: Terminology Analysis in Semantic Modeling.

Terminology analysis determines standard terms and also identifies terms that are local dialect—terms that may be recognized as synonyms or aliases but not as the enterprise standard. This is the process of defining standard vocabulary— establishing standard terms with clear definitions and descriptions and formally recognizing commonly used variations.

Terminology analysis is a crucial activity for transitioning from ontology as a knowledge graph to ontology as a semantic *model*. The semantic model is more than a diagram. It is a graph diagram plus several sets of definitions and descriptions that are produced by terminology analysis. A complete semantic ontology includes definitions and descriptions of all of the terms in the model—all labels of nodes and all labels of edges. For the knowledge graph shown here, taxonomy analysis will produce eleven sets of definitions and descriptions—five describing nodes and seven describing edges.

The emphasis on description is an important concept. Consider these definitions and descriptions:

- A **customer** is a person or organization that has placed one or more orders (current or past) through the company's e-commerce platform. Customers may include registered users with accounts as well as guest purchasers. Individuals who initiate and complete a transaction to buy goods or services are considered customers.

- An **order** is a purchase request submitted by a customer to the company for one or more products or services. Order details specify items selected, quantities, prices, delivery or pickup options, payment method, and customer obligations such as providing accurate shipping information.

- A customer **places** an order by submitting a purchase request through the e-commerce platform. The order captures the customer's intent to buy specific products or services and includes agreed-upon terms such as item selection, pricing, delivery, and payment. Once submitted, the order becomes a record of transaction and may form the basis of a sales contract.

Each of these statements is more than a simple definition. The description of customer is much more informative than the simple statement "a customer is someone who places an order." There is some depth of knowledge, and it expresses some precision and detail about what is meant by the term customer. Definition and description—not just definition. The powerful thing here is that the combination of diagram, definitions, and descriptions captures a tremendous amount of knowledge about the business, about the data, and about the language that is used—knowledge captured in an easy-to-understand diagram that is supported with a relatively modest number of words.

Properties Analysis

Analyzing properties extends the knowledge graph to become a property graph. Ask what facts are collected to identify and describe each of the nodes. Typically, each node has both identifying and descriptive properties. The properties of nodes are modeled as lists placed adjacent to the nodes that they identify and describe.

Properties analysis also asks what facts are collected to describe the edges or the relationships in the graph. With edges, we don't look for identifying properties, only for descriptive properties. In this example, delivery status and delivery timestamp describe the edge delivers that connects shipment with product. It is important in properties analysis to not only seek properties for nodes, but also ask about properties of edges.

It is also important to recognize that each property name is a new term in the model. Terminology analysis needs to be performed for properties, creating definitions and descriptions for each property name.

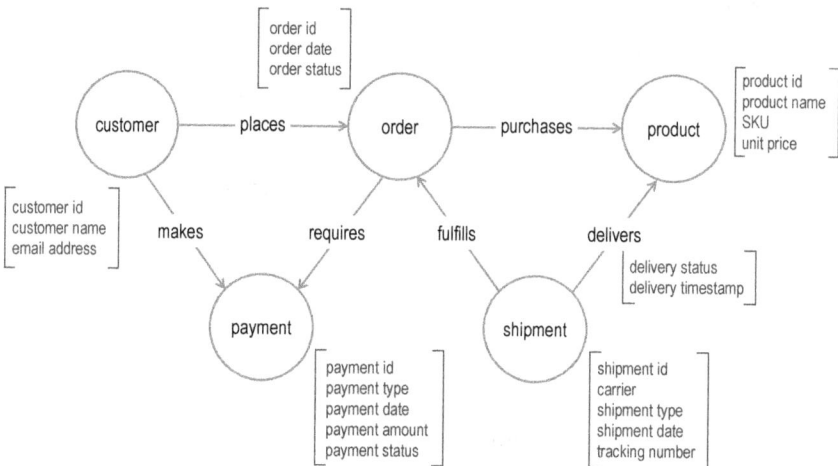

Figure 19: Ontology as a Property Graph.

Taxonomy Analysis

Analyzing taxonomies examines words and meanings from a different perspective. It is the process of organizing things that have similar qualities into named groups and standard classification structures. Taxonomy analysis asks what groups or categories exist for an entity, relationship, or property. In a data taxonomy, the categories are most commonly based on roles, types, or states. The names of the groups are additional terms to be defined and described.

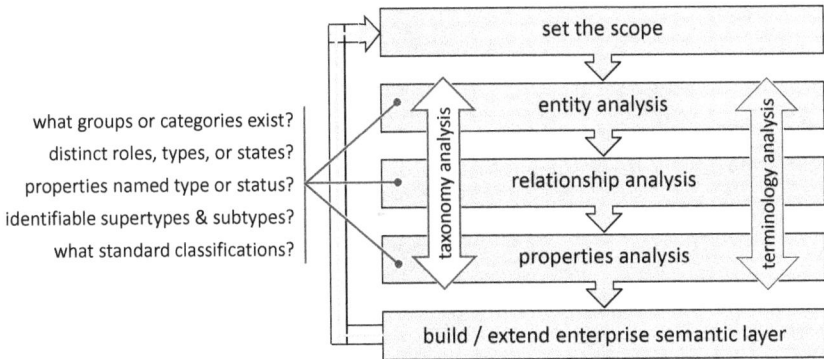

Figure 20: Taxonomy Analysis in Semantic Modeling.

Entity taxonomy is a classification of things—describing classification structures for the nodes in the graph. Examining the properties associated with each node helps to identify nodes where taxonomy analysis is needed. Property names that include words such as type, class, status, category, or group indicate probable taxonomies. The example property graph includes order status, shipment type, payment type, and payment status. This suggests one classification structure for each order and shipment, and two distinct classification structures for payment. We'll use shipment to illustrate how the property graph is extended to model entity taxonomies.

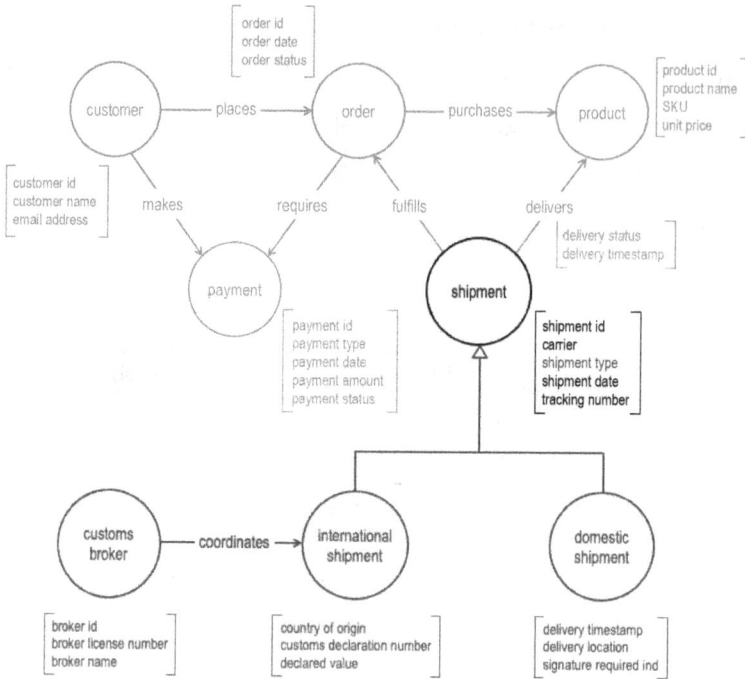

Figure 21: Entity Taxonomy Added to Property Graph.

In this example, the supertype *shipment* has two subtypes: *domestic shipment* and *international shipment*. Each of the subtypes is added as a new node in the model. And each has unique properties. International shipments have properties that don't apply for domestic shipments, and domestic shipments have properties not used internationally.

Also note that international shipments participate in a relationship that doesn't apply to domestic shipments— coordination by a customs broker. The discovery of this relationship adds a new triple to the diagram. The guideline for entity taxonomy modeling is to introduce new nodes only when some subtypes have unique attributes or participate in unique relationships. When performing taxonomy analysis, always ask the questions that help to discover unique properties and relationships. This is the iterative nature of the process, the way that the model grows as new knowledge is discovered.

Properties taxonomy describes a classification structure for attribute values. Sometimes the model has property names that include words such as type and status, but the analysis does not find subclasses with unique properties or unique relationships. These are instances where the properties taxonomy works well. Here, you see examples of payment types and payment statuses—two different ways to classify payments.

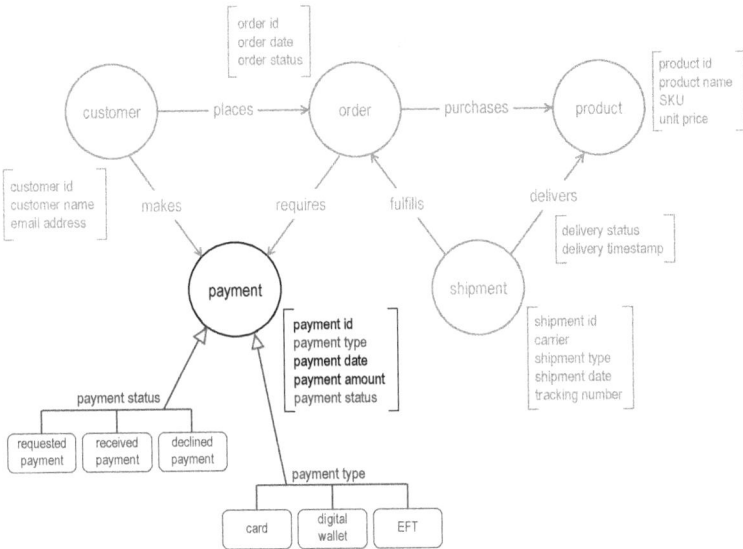

Figure 22: Properties Taxonomy in the Property Graph.

Each has subclasses, but they are subclasses without unique properties or unique relationships. Note the use of rounded rectangles instead of circles, making these subclasses visually distinct from nodes. Each term that names a subclass needs to be defined and described as part of the standard vocabulary.

Relationship taxonomy describes classification structures for the edges in a graph. Taxonomy analysis identifies relationships with potential to have subclasses—asking the question: what kinds of relationships may exist here? Sometimes properties of relationships are indicative of relationship taxonomy, and sometimes the knowledge of business SMEs is the key. Once discovered, there are three practical ways to represent them, and this is a key design decision in semantic and graph data modeling. Edge subtypes may be represented as:

- Edge properties (attributes of a relationship, such as delivery status)

- Distinct edge types (e.g., fully delivers, partially delivers, fails delivery)

- Intermediate nodes (when the relationship itself needs to be an object)

Edge properties are the simplest and most commonly used form. It is effective when the subtype variations are descriptive and not structural. Distinct edge types are useful when the subtypes represent semantically different relationships that strongly influence business decisions and practices. Intermediate nodes are well-suited when the relationship itself has an identity or a large number of attributes that need to be tracked and referenced independently.

The example shown here illustrates a properties taxonomy that is used to model the taxonomy for the shipment-delivers-product relationship.

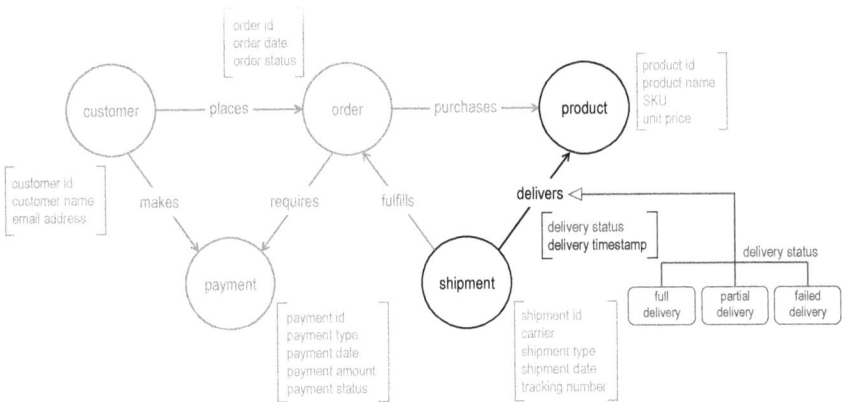

Figure 23: Relationship Classification as Property Taxonomy.

Putting the pieces together yields an extensive semantic model— comprising an ontology and taxonomies for greater depth. This example is quite a comprehensive semantic model, considering that it supports more than 50 sets of definitions and descriptions. The model describes knowledge of many different terms, with an understanding of how those terms are defined, described, and interrelated.

This small model doesn't accurately represent the scope and scale of even a very small enterprise. A typical enterprise will have dozens, perhaps hundreds, of entities and thousands of terms to define, describe, and associate. Realistically, you can't build it all at once. Think incrementally—perhaps driven by data disparity pain points, by project priorities, by critical data elements, or a combination of these things. Undertake semantic data modeling as a series of manageable projects to grow the enterprise semantic model over time.

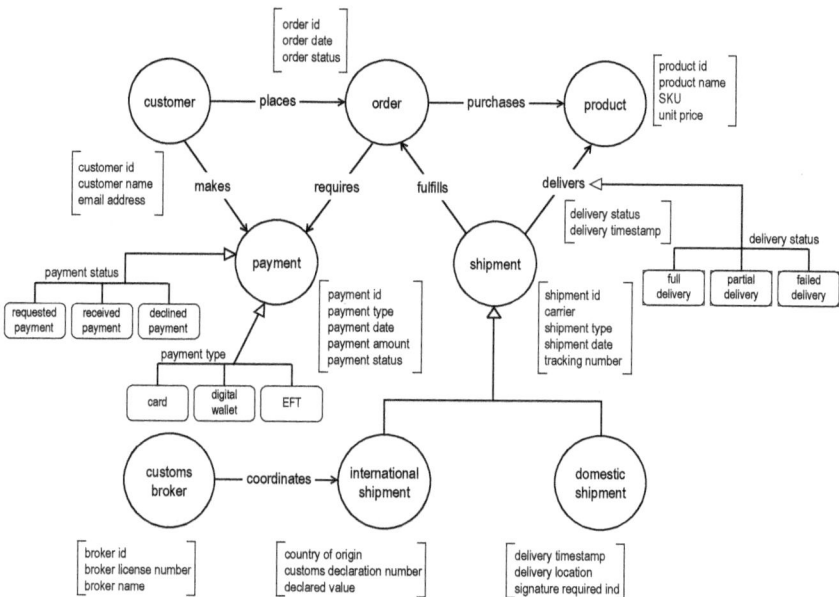

Figure 24: Semantic Data Model—Putting the Pieces Together.

When a large model becomes difficult to absorb all at once, view it in layers. Begin with the simple knowledge graph. Understand the nodes and the edges, the illustration of entities and relationships among them. Then view the property graph to understand the facts that can be known about each entity and each relationship. And finally, extend it to include taxonomies and to see classes and subclasses.

Another approach to layering begins with a knowledge graph showing entities and relationships, then adds entity taxonomies to understand the classes and subclasses of entities. Then extend it to see properties and property taxonomies, and finally any relationship-based taxonomies. The point is to capture all of the detail, all of the knowledge, all of the information that becomes available to you through semantic modeling. Don't shy away from large or complex models. Simply plan to manage the detail and complexity by layering and by segmenting diagrams. This provides the ability to look at subsets of the model without losing sight of the comprehensive view of enterprise semantics.

EIGHT

The Enterprise Semantic Layer

The enterprise semantic layer sits at the intersection of technology, meaning, and architecture. It is not a single tool or product. It is a purposeful combination of approaches working together to make data understandable and usable across the enterprise. At its core, the semantic layer creates a bridge between raw data and business context, ensuring that data from many systems can be interpreted consistently. This is achieved through a combination of data management mechanisms (APIs, data services, data products, and virtualization that are used to deliver data), along with semantic techniques (mapping, linking, and translation) that align meaning across domains.

There are many ways to implement a semantic layer, and no two organizations will do it in exactly the same way. Some will emphasize APIs and services, others will rely more heavily on virtualization or data products. Many will adopt a mix. What matters is that these methods do not exist in isolation. They are interdependent. For example, data products rely on APIs to be exposed and consumed, but not all APIs are tied to data products. Likewise, data translation depends on semantic mapping to establish equivalence, yet semantic mapping offers broader benefits such as shared vocabulary and consistency in reporting.

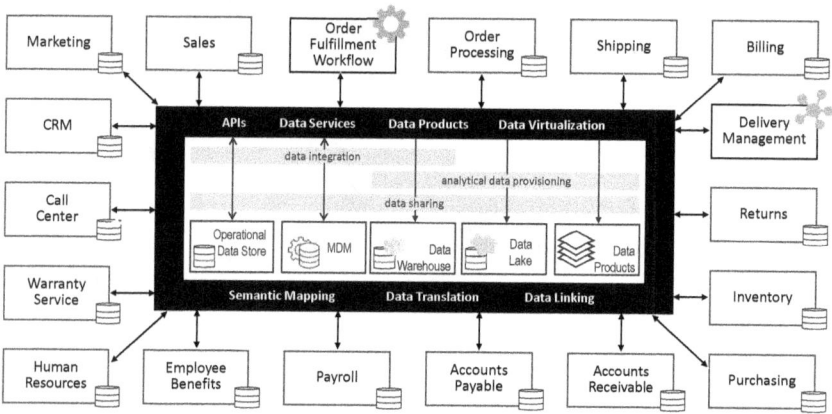

Figure 25: The Enterprise Semantic Layer in Data Management Architecture.

Because of the dependencies, every semantic layer implementation is a blend of multiple mechanisms and techniques. The choice is not about selecting a single method, but about combining the right set of capabilities to fit enterprise needs. Equally important, it is about positioning the enterprise semantic layer as a core component of the overall data management architecture. The result is a flexible, interoperable architecture where data can be delivered in meaningful, consistent ways for operational workflows, cross-domain integration, analytical processing, and AI/ML applications.

APIs and Data Services

An application programming interface (API) is a software component that acts as a communication mechanism between applications. APIs allow two applications to talk to each other. They support service-oriented communications where one application can make use of services provided by another. One application requests a service, and another responds to provide the service. An API communicates both the request and the response.

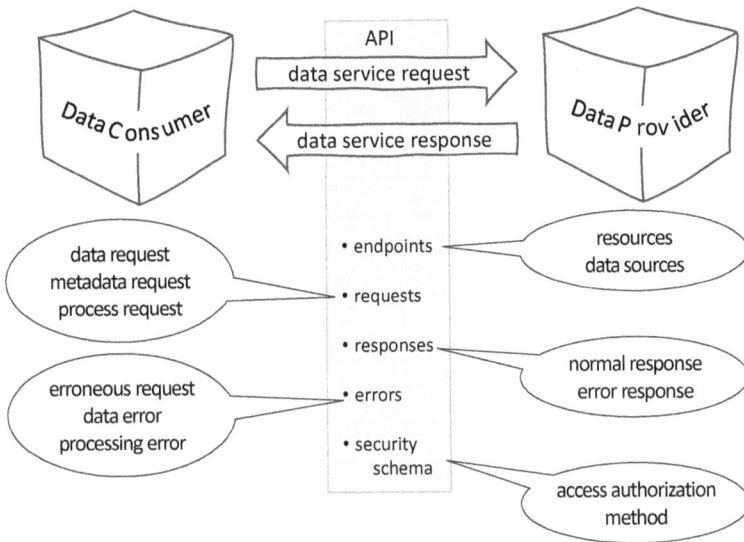

Figure 26: Data Sharing with APIs and Data Services.

When sharing data through APIs, one application has the role of data consumer and another application is the data provider. The data consumer requests data services, and the provider responds to the request. APIs for data services typically have five components:

- Endpoints are the data provider resources, the data sources that are used to provide requested data.

- Requests are data consumer calls to receive data services. Requests may ask for data, metadata, processing of data, or a combination of these.

- Responses are data provider replies to service requests, either providing the service requested or communicating an error condition.

- Errors are abnormal conditions that prevent a service request from being fulfilled. They may be erroneous requests, such as requests that don't make sense or requests for sensitive data without access authorization. They may be errors that occur when accessing data or errors that occur during data processing.

- Security schema is the data provider's mechanism to control access to protected data, the method by which the data consumer communicates authorization to access sensitive and protected data.

Ideally, data architecture provides API standards, guidelines, and design patterns that address conventions and configurations for these five API components.

Data Products

The term "data product" is used quite frequently and often without definition. To avoid ambiguity, we need to define the meaning of a data product in the context of data architecture and data interoperability.

A data product is a consumer-ready collection of accessible data that is designed to provide functionality with a specific purpose.

I believe this aligns with the more general concept of a product as something that is made or refined to provide specific functionality to meet consumer needs. A data product provides data functionality to meet the needs of data consumers. Those consumers may be human, they may be application software, or they may be analytic algorithms. The product itself consists of data, metadata, processing, and interface components. The functionality may be any of providing data, composing data from multiple sources, transforming or aggregating data, profiling data, quality checking, and so on—functions to meet the needs of data consumers.

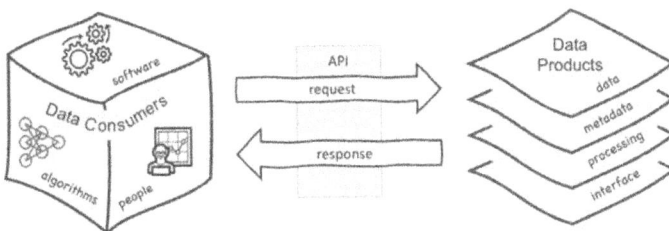

Figure 27: Data Sharing through Data Products.

The data component of a data product encompasses all types of data regardless of structure. That includes data in all of its forms—structured, unstructured, semi-structured, multi-structured, and differently structured ... tables, files, records, etc. It may be raw data, or it may be transformed, derived, or processed in other ways. It may be business data, or it may be metadata such as data profile statistics.

The metadata component includes metadata needed to understand the data—the data semantics. It may also include data privacy and sensitivity information as well as other metadata needed to guide appropriate use of data, as well as metadata describing sources and lineage of business data.

Data product processing performs the work necessary to support product functionality, including providing, composing, transforming, aggregating, profiling, and quality checking. Processing also includes security checking and verification that the consumer is authorized to access protected data, error checking and detection for the many types of errors that are possible—erroneous requests, data errors, and processing errors—and processing to compose responses for both normal and error conditions.

A data product interface may be a human user interface when data products are designed for direct human interaction. More commonly, interfaces are APIs for software interactions, and those are the interfaces that work well for data interoperability. Interfaces are the means to receive and interpret requests, provide normal responses to deliver data, and provide error responses to communicate about the nature of errors that occur.

A complete data product must include all of these components—data, metadata, processing, and interface. Without data, it is not a **data** product. Without semantic metadata, it is not understandable. Without processing to compose a response, it is pointless. And without an interface, it is inaccessible.

Regardless of function and purpose, every data product must have several characteristics to be useful, sustainable, and architecturally sound:

- **Discoverable**: Consumers can find data products through a registry or a data catalog that contains an inventory of data products and includes metadata describing each product.
- **Addressable**: Identified by a standards-based unique address that provides access by software programs.
- **Trustworthy**: Thoroughly tested and quality assured for trustworthy processing and results, and documented data lineage for trust in the data itself.
- **Self-Describing**: The functionality and the interface are clear and understandable. Data semantics provide clear, unambiguous data meaning. Interoperability standards express functionality and well-defined communication syntax.
- **Interoperable**: Able to be connected with other data, other software, and other data products based on

consistent semantics and defined standards for interoperability.

- **Secure and Governed**: With access controls and data governance constraints embedded in the product.
- **Independently Deployable**: Fully functional, free from dependencies with other data products, decoupled from and not reliant on other software components.

The power of data product architecture is amplified when data products can be interconnected—data products using the services of other data products. The characteristics of interoperability, addressability, and independent deployability are fundamental to this capability. When data products connect and communicate through their APIs, complex data services and data capabilities can be constructed as a network of data product interactions. This advanced level of data interoperability becomes possible with a well-designed and properly implemented data product architecture.

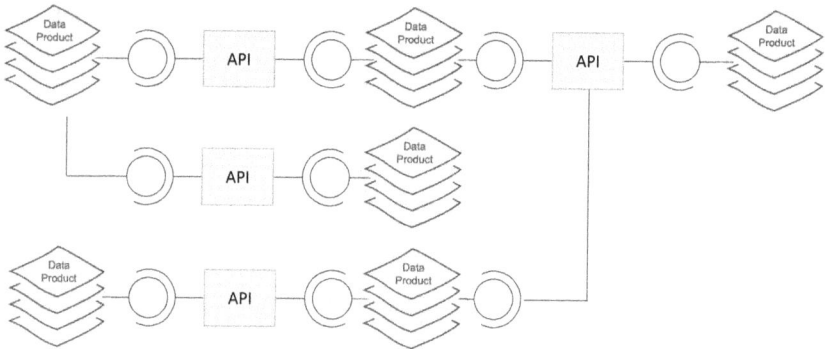

Figure 28: Data Products and Data Interoperability.

Data product architecture also provides a path to application interoperability. Application dependencies and messy point-to-point data interfaces can be replaced with a semantics-based data product approach. Semantically consistent and contractually compliant data products can be found and accessed through a searchable API registry. Applications provide data by publishing semantically conformed data products. Applications acquire the data required by accessing these semantically conforming products. Evolving from point-to-point interfaces to interoperability through data products is a practical step toward a fully functional enterprise semantic layer.

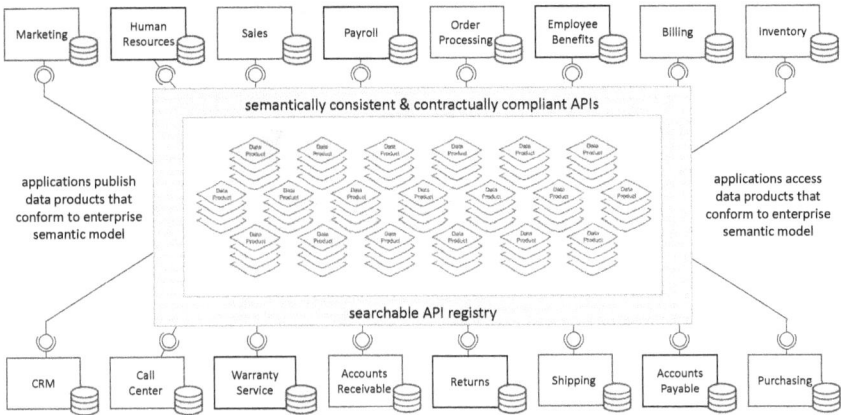

Figure 29: Data Products and Application Interoperability.

Data products are central to data mesh, which decentralizes data management to individual domains. Each domain manages its own data, publishes data products, and consumes products published by others. Enterprise views, data sharing, and remediation of data silos depend on interoperability standards to ensure that products can work together. Governance follows a federated model, with some authority centralized and some delegated to domains. Shared infrastructure—storage, pipelines, and processing—controls cost and complexity.

Interoperability standards are a cornerstone of data mesh, and their strongest expression comes through semantics. Semantics is the language of interoperability in a mesh. While data mesh is not itself a semantic layer, semantics provide the cohesion that makes product interoperability standards effective. This affinity grows even more important in hybrid architectures that blend mesh, fabric, ERP, SaaS, warehouses, and more.

> *In these contexts, the semantic layer links diverse frameworks into a unified, interoperable data environment.*

Data Contracts

Data contracts are a practical way to ensure the quality and reliability of data products and data services. A data contract specifies the structure, format, semantics, quality, and terms of use for data. Data contracts are essentially service level agreements between data providers and data consumers. Contracts define requirements for consistency and accuracy of data, regulatory compliance and protection of sensitive data, and interoperability among data products and services. A data contract may express expectations and requirements for any or all of data definitions, types, formats, structures, encodings, constraints, and quality.

A data contract is the commitment of a data product to deliver predictable results.

A data contact may be either human-readable and standards-implemented, or it may be machine readable—implemented by software and active metadata. Clearly, a machine-readable and executable data contract provides stronger enforcement than a standards-based contract. The machine-readable contract is implemented as a central component of the product delivering output or results. Executable data contracts are expressed in markup languages such as JSON and YAML.

Data Virtualization

Data virtualization provides access to data in a form that is independent of the underlying database technology, data structures, and data storage. The data is presented as an abstract layer. Wikipedia defines it as an approach to data management that enables an application to retrieve and manipulate data without requiring technical details about the data, such as its format at the source or its physical storage location.[2] Data

---

[2] https://en.wikipedia.org/wiki/Data_virtualization.

consumers request data that is returned through abstract data views. Data consumers of all types can access and blend data from various locations, structures, and across all data sources. Data is accessed in real time, without the latency inherent in ETL processing. Schemas and transformations are adaptable to individual use cases, rather than forcing data into a single rigid schema. Data blending encompasses a wide range of data types, including structured, semi-structured, multi-structured, and even some types of unstructured data. And data virtualization processes only data that is requested, in contrast with copy-based data integration, which must process all data that might be needed.

Abstraction is the nucleus of data virtualization. Layers of abstraction break down the complexities that exist when translating between consumption and storage perspectives of data.

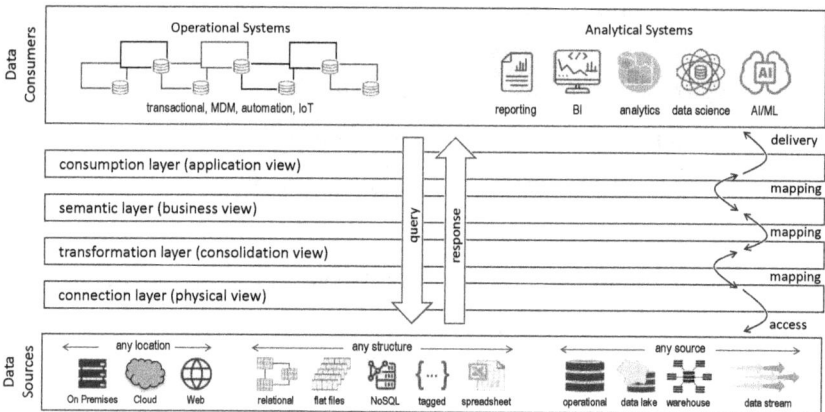

Figure 30: Data Virtualization—Layers of Abstraction.

The consumption layer is an application view of data. It describes the data in application-specific terms and organizes the data based on application-specific structure. This is the local dialect view of data.

The semantic layer is the business view of data. This may be an enterprise view when an enterprise semantic model exists, or it may be a business view of narrower scope, such as a functional area or a line of business. Mapping between the consumption and semantic layers enables the translation of queries from application context to business context, and vice versa, translating responses from business to application context.

The transformation layer is the consolidation view, bringing together data from multiple sources. Data blending and data integration are the perspectives and objectives of this layer. Data transformation logic exists and data transformation processes are executed here. Mapping between the semantic and consumption layers enables the translation of queries from the business context to the data composition context, and the description of composed data responses in the business context.

The connection layer is the physical view. It describes the location, organization, structure, access methods, and other technical details of each individual data source. Mapping between the transformation layer and the connection layer supports translation from the consolidation context to the physical views needed to access data.

The data virtualization process operates across four layers of abstraction. A consuming application initiates a query in its application language, which is progressively translated first to a semantic context, then to a transformation context, and finally to a connection context for data access. The data is processed to provide a response, progressing from physical view to consolidation view, then to business view, and finally to application view for delivery to the application.

A lot of "heavy lifting" may occur between query and response. When large amounts of data are accessed and processed, or when multiple and complex transformations are applied, query response time is likely to be affected. Most data virtualization tools include query optimizers and caching capabilities to optimize query performance.

This describes the full range of abstraction in data virtualization. It is practical and often desirable to implement with fewer layers. Delivering data as a semantic view, for example, makes sense when data consumers can interpret semantic views locally. Moving directly from the connection layer to the semantic layer makes sense for virtual data access to a single source with no need for blending, integration, and data composition. A two-layer approach mapping the connection layer to the semantic layer is practical to build the most basic virtual semantic data layer.

Data virtualization techniques can be used when building data products. The virtual data product process begins with a data consumer requesting data using semantic terminology. The semantic layer receives and interprets the request, translating it to a consolidation context to be passed to the transformation layer.

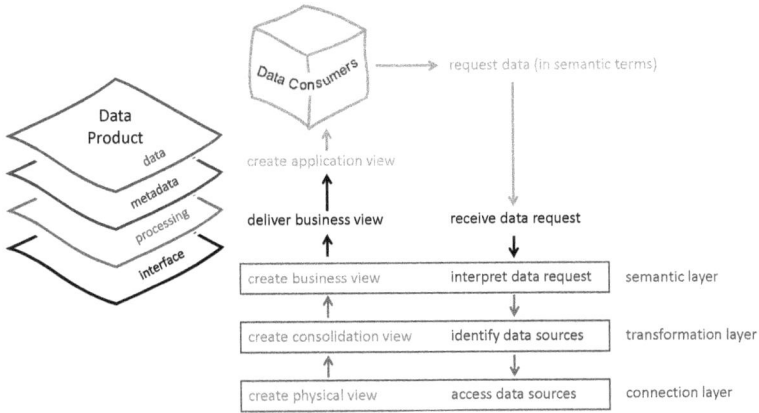

Figure 31: Data Virtualization and Data Products.

The transformation layer identifies sources and data to be accessed. Request interpretation and data source identification depend on the metadata that describes layer-to-layer mapping. Data is accessed at the connection layer, then processed through physical, consolidation, and business views, with the business view delivered to the data consumer. The data consumer may then translate data from the semantic context to the application view. Receiving the request and delivering the business view response are responsibilities of the data product's semantically compliant API.

Semantic Data Mapping

Modeling the ontology and taxonomy produces a semantic data model that provides the controlled vocabulary and standard language that is needed for data interoperability. But the semantic model alone does not create interoperability. It enables interoperability. Putting the model and the standard language to work isn't possible without first mapping local dialects—the language and terminology of the data silos—to the enterprise semantic model.

A typical operational systems environment consists of many systems, each with local terminology. Mapping each local term to a standard semantic term provides the means to translate between local dialects based on the standard language. For example, the entity that inventory calls SKU, sales refers to as item, and returns calls unit. With the semantic model expressing product as the standard term, SKU, item, and unit can all be mapped to that term. Now the inventory restocking process can communicate with the returns receiving process. Their communications are based on the standard term product, and each can locally equate that with SKU and unit. Sales can engage in similar communications, locally translating product as item.

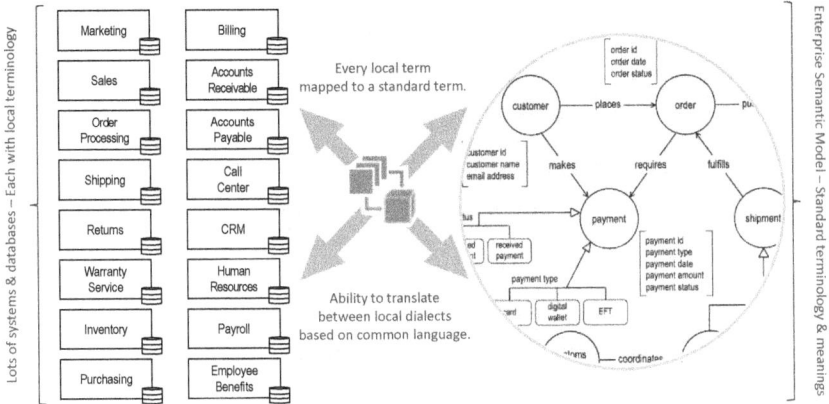

Figure 32: Mapping Local Dialects to Standard Language.

Semantic mapping can be implemented through a variety of technologies and methods, depending on the scope and complexity of the environment. Rule-based mapping tools allow stewards to define equivalences between local terms and standard semantic terms, often through configuration in a metadata repository or data catalog. Schema-matching and ontology-alignment tools use pattern recognition, similarity scoring, or natural language processing to suggest mappings automatically, which subject matter experts can then validate.

In some cases, mappings are expressed formally using RDF/OWL, SKOS, or other semantic web standards, which make them reusable and machine-interpretable. Other implementations rely on transformation logic built into integration platforms, data services, or APIs, where mappings are embedded in the rules that convert source data into standard representations. Machine learning approaches are also emerging, especially for unstructured or weakly-structured data, where algorithms can infer likely mappings from context or usage patterns.

Across all these methods, the key is that mappings must be explicit, documented, and maintained.

They form the operational bridge between the enterprise semantic model and the local dialects of individual systems, enabling the interoperability that the semantic layer promises.

Data Translation

Data consumers—both people and processes—often use entirely different data language than the suppliers of data. Without a semantic layer, translation between data dialects is embedded in the code of consumer requests, supplier responses, or both. With a semantic data model and semantic mapping in place, it is practical to implement data translation capabilities as executable software.

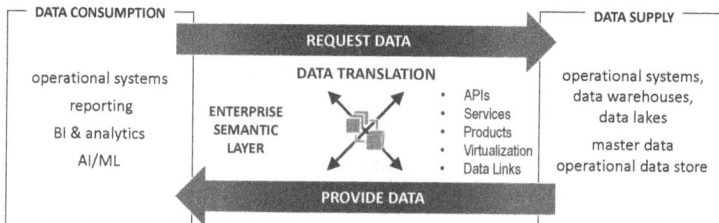

Figure 33: Data Translation In the Semantic Layer.

The enterprise semantic layer contains data translators—the software components to perform data translations. Consumer requests for data are passed to suppliers via the semantic layer. Data acquired from suppliers is routed to consumers through the semantic layer. With a well-designed semantic layer, the translation can be built in a variety of ways, including APIs, data services, data products, data virtualization, and data links. The translation is reliable, reusable, and consistent when built into the semantic layer.

Data Linking

Data linking is one of the most powerful ways to implement interoperability. Instead of copying or consolidating data into yet another repository, links make information usable where it resides. A link can be as simple as a structural connection—an API call, a reference in a master identifier, or a federated query—or as advanced as a semantic assertion that expresses how one dataset relates to another.

> *What makes links so valuable is that they reduce redundancy, preserve lineage, and allow systems to work with each other in real time, without the brittleness of point-to-point integrations.*

Different approaches to linking reinforce this capability in different ways. Some create a universal "fabric" of dataset interoperability, where each dataset is discoverable and accessible regardless of its storage or format. Others focus on zero-copy access, allowing consumers to use source data directly while preserving governance, controls, and semantics. Still others build links at the semantic level, with RDF and OWL expressing meaning through triples, vocabularies, and ontologies. In these cases, a link is not just a pointer—it is also a statement of meaning, ensuring that "customer" in one system and "buyer" in another can be recognized as the same concept.

Graph databases extend this linking paradigm by making relationships a first-class data asset. Whether as RDF triple stores or property graphs, they represent and query the network of connections across systems, domains, and datasets. This ability to store, traverse, and reason over links provides a durable foundation for interoperability, especially when combined with semantic standards. Graph models align naturally with the enterprise semantic layer, turning data links into reusable assets that span architectures and enable consistent interpretation across operational, analytical, and hybrid environments.

NINE

Interoperability in the Data Management Architecture

The semantic layer is the nucleus of data interoperability. It is the middleware that implements data translation capabilities, making it possible for diverse applications to communicate seamlessly. App-to-app data communications can be implemented without awkward transitions, interruptions, or misunderstandings. Data consumers initiate data requests in their local language. The semantic layer translates to standard vocabulary that is understood by data providers. Providers respond in standard language, which is then translated back to application language by the semantic layer.

Semantic modeling, data mapping, and APIs form the foundation of a semantic layer. Semantic modeling is the means to develop a standard vocabulary. Data mapping refers to the relationships between application languages and the standard language—the connections that form the core of translation capabilities. APIs are the semantically compliant interfaces that prescribe the form, structure, and content of app-to-app communications.

Building on the modeling, mapping, and interface foundation, a semantic layer is implemented with data products, data contracts, data links, and data virtualization—typically a combination of several or all of these methods.

Tools and Technologies

The implementation methods—data products, data contracts, data links, and data virtualization —don't work without supporting technology. Many different kinds of technologies can be used and combined to implement a semantic data layer.

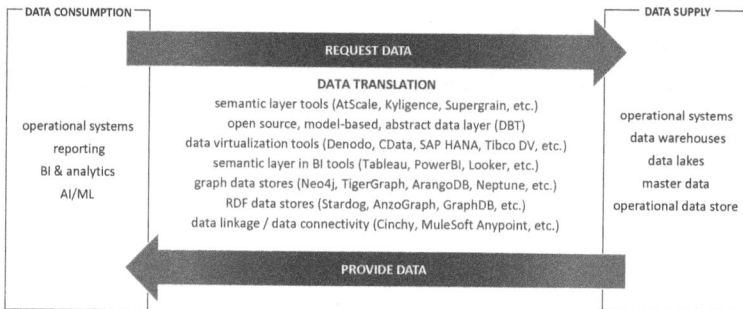

DATA CONSUMPTION	DATA TRANSLATION	DATA SUPPLY
	REQUEST DATA	
operational systems reporting BI & analytics AI/ML	semantic layer tools (AtScale, Kyligence, Supergrain, etc.) open source, model-based, abstract data layer (DBT) data virtualization tools (Denodo, CData, SAP HANA, Tibco DV, etc.) semantic layer in BI tools (Tableau, PowerBI, Looker, etc.) graph data stores (Neo4j, TigerGraph, ArangoDB, Neptune, etc.) RDF data stores (Stardog, AnzoGraph, GraphDB, etc.) data linkage / data connectivity (Cinchy, MuleSoft Anypoint, etc.)	operational systems data warehouses data lakes master data operational data store
	PROVIDE DATA	

Figure 34: Data Translation Technologies.

Semantic layer technologies implement a semantic layer as middleware. They sit between data consumers that request data and data suppliers that provide data. I'll mention a few specific technologies here as examples, but I want to be clear that these are examples and not product recommendations or endorsements, and that they are current at the time of this writing, but we live in a world of continuously evolving technologies.

Semantic layer tools are one type of data translation technology. These are built specifically for semantic data translations and include tools such as AtScale, Kyligence, and Supergrain. Open-source, model-based tools such as DBT can be used to build a semantics-based abstract data layer. Data virtualization tools, such as Denodo, CData, and SAP HANA, also provide data abstraction, as described earlier. BI tools like Tableau, PowerBI, and Looker include semantic layer capabilities that have somewhat limited reach but can be part of implementing an enterprise semantic layer.

Graph data stores inherently implement ontology as described with knowledge graphs and property graphs. Neo4j, TigerGraph, ArrangoDB, and Neptune are examples of graph data stores. RDF stores such as Stardog, AnzoGraph, and GraphDB also implement ontologies as triples. Data linkage and connectivity tools describe data relationships in a way similar to hyperlinks describing document relationships. Cinchy, and MuleSoft Anypoint are examples of data linkage.

So, semantic layer technologies are abundant, with lots of choices and lots of variety. You won't need all of them, but it is unlikely that you'll build an enterprise semantic layer using only one. Tool interoperability, metadata sharing, compatibility with existing technology infrastructure, and the fit into a technology roadmap are important considerations when choosing tools.

Adapting Your Architecture for Interoperability

Data semantics is a concept and viewpoint to enable data interoperability. A semantic data layer is a core component of data management architecture. Building a semantic layer makes substantial changes to your data management architecture. You already have data management architecture. That means that implementing a semantic layer is not design of a new architecture, but a process of adapting existing architecture. Plan to adapt systematically and with a minimum of disruption by asking several questions:

- What architecture do you have? Knowing the starting point is essential—understanding the architectural structure that will be modified to include a semantic layer as a new component. What operational systems, operational data stores, data warehouses, data marts, and data lakes do you have? How are they related and interconnected? A data architecture diagram is especially useful here.

- What new capabilities will you add with a semantic layer? What problems will be solved? State your

objectives for data semantics—breaking down data silos,
resolving semantic inconsistencies, reducing point-to-
point interfaces, finding and managing data
redundancies, etc.

- What techniques and technologies will you use to build a
  semantic layer? Semantic modeling, semantic mapping,
  and APIs are interoperability cornerstones. What about
  data products, data contracts, graph stores, RDF stores,
  and data links?

- How will you modify your architecture? What new
  components and configurations? What will be added,
  what will change, and what will be removed? How will it
  all fit together? Again, an architecture diagram is
  especially helpful.

How will you implement changes to data management
architecture and data management practices? Gradual migration,
incremental change, big bang? The design of architecture is only
the beginning.

---

*Putting it into practice—getting people to use it and to
apply the techniques, the tools, and the standards—that's
the real work of architecture implementation. That's how
you'll achieve the data interoperability goals—breaking
down silos, eliminating point-to-point interfaces, resolving
semantic inconsistency, and so on.*

Before Interoperability

Putting the pieces together, let's examine an example of adapting data management architecture by introducing data semantics to achieve data interoperability. This diagram illustrates data management before the addition of semantic capabilities and the implementation of data interoperability.

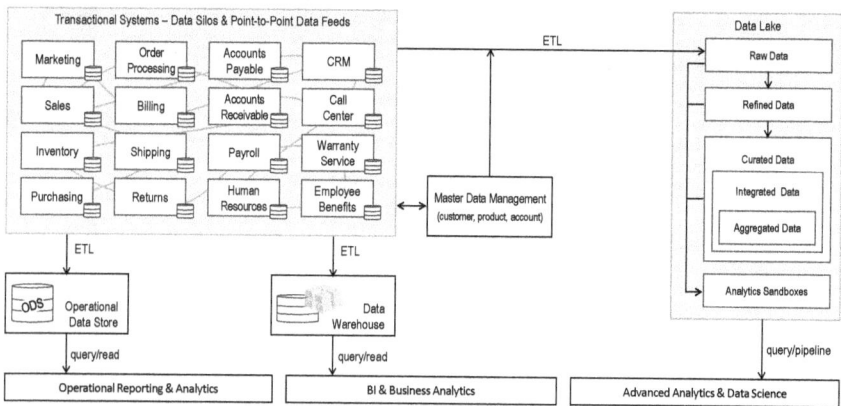

Figure 35: Data Architecture Before Data Interoperability.

Transactional systems, in the upper left, are a collection of data silos that communicate and exchange data through a complex assortment of single-purpose, point-to-point data feeds.

ETL processes extract data from these systems and transform it for consistency of meaning, structure, and encodings, and then load it into an operational data store. The ODS is a source of integrated operational data used for operational reporting and operational analytics.

Another set of ETL processes extracts data from transactional systems and transforms it to resolve redundancy and disparity. Consistency of meaning, structure, and encodings is again a goal of the processing, but the transformations are not entirely aligned with those for the operational data store. This second set of ETL processing fits data to a data warehouse schema and loads data into the warehouse. Warehouse data is consumed by business intelligence and analytics applications.

At this point, we have transactional data silos, an ODS, and a data warehouse. The origins of this legacy data architecture—ODS and warehouse integration—can be traced back to nearly 30 years in the past. It provides data for reporting, BI, and analytics applications that are still in use today. Several years later, data architecture was extended to include master data management. MDM provides "golden records" that contain consistent, non-redundant data for customers, products, and accounts. MDM improved data consistency and data sharing among transactional systems, but did not eliminate data silos or point-to-point data feeds.

Big data adoption, along with demand for self-service data, brought data lake concepts to data management. The data lake provides data for advanced analytics and data science. But it also adds another set of ETL processing to ingest data from transactional systems. The ODS, data warehousing, and a data lake contain independent copies of the same operational and transactional data. This means a relatively high burden of ETL processing for transactional systems, potential for inconsistencies among multiple copies of data, and uncertainty for data engineers and data scientists when choosing data sources.

With Interoperability

The updated architecture represents a fundamental shift from point-to-point integration and siloed data exchanges to an interoperability-first approach. The direct connections between operational systems have been eliminated, replaced by a framework of data products managed within their respective domains. Each domain now owns and publishes its data products—designed around business meaning and governed by enterprise interoperability standards—while also consuming products from other domains as needed. This shift decentralizes data management but ensures consistency through shared semantics, giving domains both autonomy and alignment.

Although the semantic layer is not explicitly drawn in the diagram, it is central to the design. Data products are built on APIs and services that comply with semantics-based interoperability standards, enabling them to work together seamlessly regardless of their originating systems. The semantic layer thus operates behind the scenes, ensuring that when one domain publishes a product, another domain can use it without ambiguity or translation failures. In this way, semantics provides the cohesion that makes domain data management viable at enterprise scale.

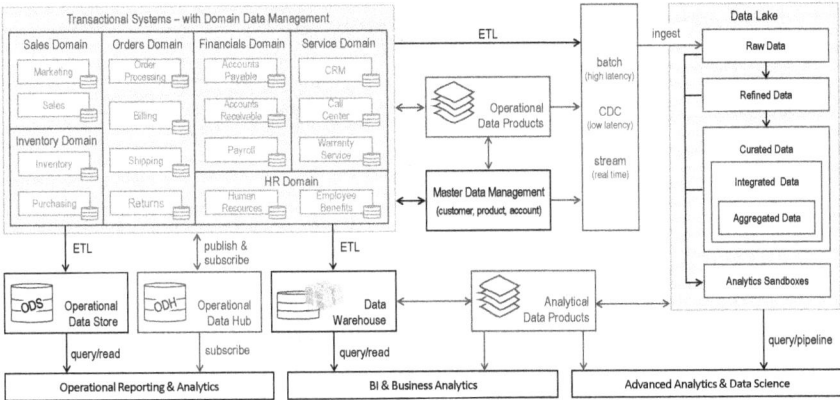

Figure 36: Data Architecture with Data Interoperability.

Importantly, the transformation does not require abandoning existing capabilities. Operational reporting, business intelligence, data warehousing, and data lake analytics continue to function as before. The architecture is evolutionary rather than revolutionary, allowing incremental implementation without disruption of current capabilities. Over time, as more domains expose standards-based data products, reliance on brittle ETL pipelines and siloed feeds diminishes, replaced by a flexible, sustainable framework for enterprise data use.

This transition illustrates the real promise of data interoperability. It demonstrates how a semantic layer, implemented largely through data products and standardized APIs, enables systems to connect without sacrificing local autonomy or enterprise cohesion. By removing the technical debt of point-to-point feeds while preserving the strengths of existing architectures, interoperability offers both stability and adaptability. It is a logical conclusion: data semantics and interoperability are not bolt-ons but the foundation for future-ready enterprise data architecture.

Final Thoughts

The future of enterprise data is not about building bigger warehouses, more pipelines, or larger lakes—it is about making data understandable and usable wherever it lives. The semantic layer provides the common language, and data products provide the delivery mechanism. Together, they transform fragmented systems into a connected ecosystem, where domains manage their own data but share it in ways others can trust and use.

Interoperability is not a one-time project or a disruptive overhaul; it is an architectural capability that grows stronger with each new data product and standard adopted. The result is an enterprise where data flows freely, decisions are made with confidence, and change is easier to absorb. By embracing semantics, links, mappings, and data products, organizations build not just a modern data architecture but a resilient foundation for the next generation of analytics, automation, and intelligence.

Index